The Story of

Inventions

"Cyrus McCormick Invents the Reaper"

By

Michael J. McHugh
Frank P. Bachman

—Table of Contents—

Chapter	Pages
Preface	v

– PART ONE –

Chapter	Pages
1 James Watt and the Invention of the Steam Engine	1-24
2 Robert Fulton and the Invention of the Steamboat	25-54
3 George Stephenson and the Invention of the Locomotive	55-82
4 Invention of the Electric Engine and Electric Locomotive	83-100

– PART TWO –

Chapter	Pages
5 The Invention of Spinning Machines	101-120
6 Eli Whitney and the Invention of the Cotton Gin	121-140
7 Elias Howe and the Invention of the Sewing Machine	141-168
8 Cyrus H. McCormick and the Invention of the Reaper	169-192
9 Henry Bessemer and the Making of Steel	193-222

Chapter	Pages

– PART THREE –

10 John Gutenberg and the Invention of
      Printing   223-246
11 Samuel F.B. Morse and the Invention of
      the Telegraph   247-270
12 Alexander Graham Bell and the Invention 271-294
      of the Telephone

– PART FOUR –

13 Thomas A. Edison   295-304
14 Orville and Wilbur Wright   305-314
15 Guglielmo Marconi   315-320
16 John L. Baird and the Invention of the 321-326
      Television
17 John P. Holland and the Submarine   327-334
18 Wernher Von Braun and Rockets to the 335-345
      Moon
19 The Invention of the Computer   346-353

Preface

This book contains numerous stories regarding the development of great inventions. The story of each invention is often interwoven with insights into the life of its inventor. This reading material is not only interesting, but helps to convey vivid lessons about how major inventions were made, and on the character traits that each inventor had to employ to achieve success.

It is hoped that this book will help young people to think about how the modern conveniences of life have been created, and how progress has been made in the industrial world. Hopefully, the youngsters who read this book will come into contact with some idea or principle that will grip their hearts, and mold their ideals into worthier forms.

Instructors are encouraged to remind their students that although most of the inventions described in this reader have changed or matured since their development, it is still helpful for young people to understand the historical origins of many of the inventions that they use every day.

Finally, each instructor is encouraged to remind their students that it was the Lord Jesus Christ who gave the creative genius to each of the inventors mentioned in this text. All glory belongs to God for giving the world wisdom and knowledge.

Michael J. McHugh
Arlington Heights, Illinois

A PUBLICATION OF
Christian Liberty Press

GREAT INVENTIONS OF THE PAST

The Story of Inventions

America's industrial buildup, which began in the late 19th century, was rapid and dramatic. Among the many important contributors to the process was Henry Ford. His introduction of the Model T in 1914 put America on wheels, and his assembly line system of manufacture revolutionized production methods.

PART 1

Inventions of Steam and Electric Power

Chapter 1

James Watt and the Invention of the Steam Engine

Until a little more than two hundred years ago, the chief power used in the production of food, clothing, and shelter was hand power. Cattle and horses were used to cultivate the fields. Windmills and water wheels were employed to grind corn and wheat. But most tools and machines were worked by hand.

JAMES WATT

Men had, for many years, dreamed of a new power that would be more useful than work

1

animals, sails, windmills, or water wheels. Around the year 1750, a new power was found. This new power was steam. Yet no one had been able to apply the power of steam to grind corn and wheat, or spin and weave cotton and wool, or do anything useful at all. The man who succeeded in giving this new power to the world was James Watt. Thanks to the efforts of Mr. Watt, the power of steam was harnessed and by the mid-1800's was propelling large ships around the world and operating hundreds of steam-powered express trains. Numerous other inventions were created from steam power as well. Although we seldom think of steam power today, we must not forget how much it helped America years ago.

Childhood and Early Education

James Watt was born in 1736, at Greenock, Scotland, not far from Glasgow. His early education was received at home, his mother giving him lessons in reading, and teaching him to draw with pencil and chalk. His father drilled him in arithmetic and encouraged him in the use of tools. A few years later James went to school, although he did not at first get along well. This was due to illness, which often kept him at home for weeks at a time. Still, he always did well in arithmetic and geometry, and after the age of fourteen he made rapid progress in all his studies.

WATT AND THE TEAKETTLE

Even as a small boy, James liked to tinker with things. This tinkering was not always appreciated by members of his family. His aunt would scold him: "James Watt, I never saw such an idle boy; read a book or employ yourself usefully; for the last hour you have not spoken a word, but taken off the lid of that kettle and put it on again. Why are you holding a cup and then a silver spoon over the steam while staring at the drops of water it turns into? Are you not ashamed to spend your time in this way?"

Much of his time, as he grew older and stronger, was spent in his father's shop, where supplies for ships were kept, and where ship repairing was done. He had a small forge and also a workbench of his own. Here he made cranes, pulleys, and pumps, and learned to work with different metals and woods. He was so skillful that the men remarked, "James has a fortune at his fingers' ends."

The time at last came for choosing a trade. His father had wished James to follow him in his own business. But Mr. Watt had recently lost considerable money, and it now seemed best for the youth to choose a trade in which he could use his mechanical talents. So James travelled to the city of Glasgow to become an instrument maker.

Learning Instrument Making

He began to work for a mechanic who dignified himself with the name of "optician." This mechanic, though the best in Glasgow, was a sort of Jack-of-all-trades, who earned a simple living by mending glasses, repairing fiddles, and making fishing tackle. Watt was useful enough to his master, but there was little that a skillful boy could learn from such a workman. So he decided to seek a teacher in London.

There were plenty of instrument makers in London, but they were bound together in a guild. A boy wishing to learn the trade must train from five to seven years. Watt had no desire to bind himself for so long a period. He wished to learn what he needed to know in the shortest possible time; he wanted a "short cut." Master workman after master workman for this reason turned him away. Only after many weeks did he find a master teacher who was willing to take him. For a year's instruction, he paid one hundred dollars and agreed to work without pay for one year.

The hours in the London shops were long. "We work," wrote Watt, "until nine o'clock every night, except Saturdays." To relieve his father of the burden of supporting him, he got up early and did extra work.

Towards the end of the year he wrote, with no little pride: "I shall be able to get my bread anywhere, as I am now able to work as well as most journeymen, though I am not so quick as many."

Jack-Of-All-Trades

In order to open a shop of his own, Watt returned to Glasgow. He was opposed in this by the hammermen's guild. The hammermen said that he had not served an apprenticeship and had no right to begin a business. They would have succeeded in keeping him from making a start, had not a friend, a teacher in the University of Glasgow, come to his aid, providing him with a shop in a small room of one of the college buildings.

Watt soon became a Jack-of-all-trades. He cleaned and repaired instruments for the university. Falling into the ways of his first master, he made and sold eyeglasses and fishing tackle. Though he had no ear for music and scarcely knew one note from another, he tried his hand at making organs. He was so successful that many "dumb flutes and gouty harps, dislocated violins, and fractured guitars" came to him to be cured of their ills.

All the while, Watt spent his leisure time in reading. The college library was close at hand, so there was no lack of books. He studied chemistry, mathematics, and mechanics. By learning all he could and by doing everything well, Watt came to be known as a man "who knew much and who could make anything."

Captured By Steam

Coal and tin mining had for a long time been important industries in Great Britain. Shallow mines were easy to work. Men and women carried out the coal or tin ore in buckets, by winding stairs. Or a windlass was used, turned by hand or with the aid of a horse. Water was taken out in the same way. As the shallow mines became exhausted, deeper ones were opened. The deeper the mine, the harder it was to lift out the coal or tin ore. Into

these deeper mines also came quantities of water, flooding many of them. Unless a machine could be invented to easily and cheaply pump out the water and hoist the coal or tin, these mines would have to be closed. The need for such a machine led to the invention of the first successful steam engine.

Watt first heard of the steam engine in 1759. The idea captivated him, and he began to read how others had tried to make successful engines. Finding that the best books on steam and "fire engines," as they were then called, were in Italian and German, he began the study of these languages.

In an Italian book he read about Branca's steam engine, invented in 1629. Branca's engine was little more than a toy, no use being made of it, except to pulverize saltpeter and do other simple things of a similar sort.

In a German book he read about Papin's engine, which was invented in 1690. In Papin's engine, steam was admitted into the cylinder. The steam was then allowed to condense, that is, turn back into water. This formed a vacuum, a space without any air in it, under the piston. The weight of the atmosphere, which is about fourteen pounds per square inch, on

BRANCA'S STEAM ENGINE OF 1629

the upper side of the piston, forced it down, and the descending piston raised a weight fastened to the rope. Papin never went further than the making of a model. But his ideas of using steam to make a vacuum, and using the pressure of the atmosphere to force down a piston were applied a few years later with some success by Thomas Newcomen.

Newcomen made his first engine in 1705. Although big and awkward, a number were used in England to pump water out of the mines. But they could not be used in deep mines, as they could lift only six or seven pounds for each square inch of the piston. They worked slowly,

NEWCOMEN'S ENGINE

9

making only about fifteen strokes a minute. They were also expensive to operate, a single engine burning several thousand dollars' worth of coal in a month.

Finding the Trouble

Watt had been thinking about steam for four or five years before he saw one of Newcomen's engines. It was only a model of one, brought to him from the university for repair. When he had repaired the model, he started it up one more time. It made a few strokes and stopped. There was no more steam. The boiler seemed big enough, so he started a bigger fire. The engine now ran all right, but it required much fuel and used up quantities of steam, though the load on the side of the pump was light. Most men would have thought nothing of this, and would have sent the model back to the university. But that was not Watt's way. Everything he did not understand was for him a subject for study, and he never stopped until he understood. So he began to work to discover why the engine used so much steam.

Steam was used, you will remember, to make a vacuum in the cylinder. Watt found that to drive out the air and water, enough steam had to be let into the cylinder to fill it four times. Why was this? First, the cylinder was exposed to the air, which chilled it. The cold cylinder itself, before it was warm, changed considerable steam into water. Second, cold water was poured into the cylinder to condense the steam, and this made the cylinder cold again. Watt estimated that three fourths of all the steam used was thus wasted in heating and reheating the cylinder. Here was the trouble with Newcomen's engine. Watt saw that, to remedy this defect, a way must be found to keep the cylinder always as hot as the steam which entered it, and the vacuum must be made in the cylinder, without cooling it.

Making the Invention

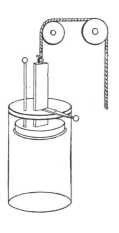

Watt spent much time and money in making experiments, but nothing he tried succeeded. "Nature has a weak side," he was fond of saying, "if we can only find it out." So he went on day after day, following one false hope after another.

"One Sunday afternoon early in 1765," writes Watt, "I had gone to take a walk in the parks of Glasgow. I was thinking about the engine and how to save the heat in the cylinder, when the idea came into my mind that steam was an elastic body and would run into a vacuum. If connection was made between the cylinder and a tank from which the air had been pumped, the steam would pass into the empty tank and might there be condensed without cooling the cylinder. I then saw that I must get rid of the condensed steam and the water used to produce it. It occurred to me that this could be done by using pumps."

With a separate condenser in mind, to get rid of the steam after it had done its work, without cooling the cylinder, other important improvements were thought of. In Newcomen's engine, the upper end of the cylinder was open to let the air act upon the piston. Watt now planned to put an air-tight cover over the end of the cylinder, with a hole for the piston rod to slide through, and to let steam in above the piston to act upon it, instead of the air. This change turned Newcomen's atmospheric engine into a steam engine. In Newcomen's engine, the power was the pressure of the atmosphere upon the piston, and this power acted in one direction only. In Watt's engine, steam was the power, and the piston was shoved both up and down by it; hence Watt's engine was called a double-acting engine.

"All these improvements," says Watt, "followed . . . in quick succession, so that in the course of one or two days the invention was . . . complete in my mind."

The next step was to make a model, so the invention could be put into working form. Making the drawings was easy, but to carry them out was hard. A lack of good workmen was the main difficulty. There were no skilled mechanics in those days, nor automatic tool-making machines; everything had to be made by hand. Blacksmiths and tinners were the only men that could be hired, and they were bungling workers even at their own trades. After eight months of racking labor, the model was ready to start. It worked, but despite all Watt's efforts, it "sniffed at many joints." The condenser did not work well; the cylinder leaked, and the

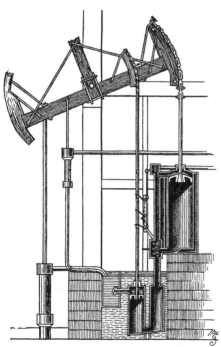

THE ENGINE BEELZEBUB, 1767

piston was far from being steamtight. To add to Watt's troubles, his "old White Iron man," a tinner who was his best workman, died. The crossbeam on the engine also broke. Nevertheless, Watt saw enough to know that he was on the right track.

Beelzebub, the Trial Engine

Watt's great need was money, for it was necessary to build a trial engine to show the value of steam power. Finally, in 1767, he secured a partner who promised, for a two-thirds share in the invention, to pay a debt of five thousand dollars owed by Watt, and to bear the expense of further experiments. The partnership was formed, and Watt turned to the plans for the trial engine.

As the trial engine neared completion, Watt's "anxiety for his approaching doom kept him sleepless at night, for his fears were even greater than his hopes." Alas! the trial engine did not work well. The new condenser worked badly. The cylinder was almost useless. The piston, despite all that could be done, leaked quantities of steam. The whole machine was a "clumsy job." From the way it wheezed, and snorted, and puffed fire and smoke, the engine was named Beelzebub. Months were spent in overhauling him, but he behaved only slightly better during the second trial. Beelzebub was far from being a practical engine, and he was left for the time to rest and rust.

There is little wonder that Watt was downhearted and wrote to his friends: "Of all things in life, there is nothing more foolish than inventing." "I am resolved . . . if I can resist it, to invent no more." "Today I enter the

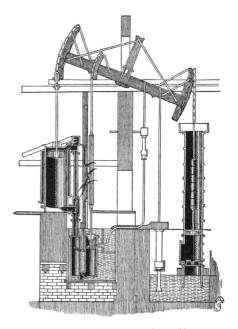

thirty-fifth year of my life, and I think I have hardly yet done thirty-four cents worth of good in the world."

Completing the Engine

Watt had by this time spent ten years and several thousand dollars on his invention, but it was still only a dream. Brighter days were, however, at hand. Matthew Boulton, owner of the largest hardware factory in England and employer of the best mechanics in Europe, became interested in the fire engine. In 1774 he became Watt's partner.

Meanwhile, old Beelzebub was shipped to Birmingham.

The best mechanics of Soho began to work upon him. One by one the separate parts were repaired and improved. In a few months, he was ready for trial. Beelzebub puffed as much smoke and fire as ever, but he worked surprisingly well thanks to good workmanship of the mechanics. Everyone who saw Beelzebub run felt sure that the invention would prove a success. Even modest Watt wrote to his father: "The fire engine I have invented is now going, and works much better than any other that has yet been made, and I expect that the invention will be very beneficial to me."

Though success was promised, much remained to be done to make the engine practical. It was found, for example, that if the load Beelzebub was pulling suddenly became lighter, he would run too fast; if the load suddenly became heavier, he would run too slow.

Some way had to be found to make him run faster when there was need of more power, and to run more slowly when less power was needed. Two heavy balls were fixed to swing around an upright rod. When the engine ran fast, the upright rod turned fast, and the balls swung out and directed the engine to admit less steam. When the engine ran slowly, the rod turned slowly, and the balls swung down and let in more steam. By the use of this contrivance called a governor, Beelzebub was made to run at consistent speed, and when in operation, became his own engineer.

Other inventions were made, and the separate condenser, piston, and cylinder were improved. Thus, after years of thought and labor, the steam engine at length stood full-grown and ready for all kinds of work.

Making the Business Pay

To make an invention is one thing. To get people to use it and so make it profitable is another. It is difficult to say which is the harder. In any case, Watt's troubles were not over.

All the time that Watt was working on his invention, mines were being abandoned because they had become flooded with water. Among the first orders for engines was one for a mine in Cornwall. Watt made the drawing with care, and the workmen did their best, for much depended on the first engine for their future success.

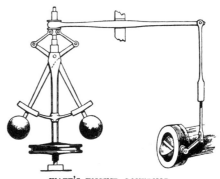

WATT'S ENGINE GOVERNOR

The engine was ready by

the middle of 1777, and Watt went to set it up. The people were eager to get a look at the monster. Mine owners came from far and near to see it work. Many were doubtful, and some even wished that the engine might fail. But to the surprise of all, it succeeded. It pumped water as they had never seen water pumped before. The size, the speed, and "the horrible noise of the engine," wrote Watt, "give satisfaction . . . and the noise seems to give great ideas of its powers." In a few days the mine was dry. It was the deepest mine in the district, and orders for engines began to pour in. They came so fast that in the course of the next four or five years almost all the mines in England and Scotland were supplied.

Boulton, Watt's partner, felt from the first that the greatest field for the steam engine was in mills and factories. When orders for pumping engines fell off, Watt went to work on a factory engine. He built his first factory engine in 1782, and it was for a corn mill.

The use of the steam engine in mills was opposed by the millers. They realized that if steam engines were permitted to grind corn and wheat, they would do away in many places with windmills and water mills. The working people also were stirred up. They were led to believe that if the steam engine was put in mills, it would take work away from them.

"It seems," wrote Watt, "the meddlers are determined to be masters of us. To put a stop to fire-engine mills, because they come in competition with water mills, would be as absurd as to put a stop to canals, because they interfere with wagoners. . . . The argument that men are deprived of a livelihood would put a stop to the use of all machines whereby labor is saved. Carry out this argument, and we must do away with water mills themselves, and go back again to grinding corn by hand labor."

So strong was the opposition that Watt and Boulton decided to build a flour mill, to show what could be done. They built one at a cost of sixty thousand dollars, and put into it their newest and best engine. The mill attracted much attention. But it was not allowed to run long. So bitter was the feeling against the steam engine that the mill was set on fire and burned to the ground.

Though the mill was a total loss, it served its purpose. Orders for factory engines came in rapidly from France, from Italy, and from America. The advantages of steam power were now apparent to some people. Water mills were stopped in the summer by lack of water, and in the winter by frost, while steam mills worked on, day and night, in all kinds of weather, and in all seasons.

To bring the world to appreciate the value of the steam engine was, therefore, a hard struggle. Until the year 1785 every penny made from the sale of engines, amounting to more than two hundred thousand dollars, was put back into the business. Besides, large sums were borrowed. So great was the need for money that even the patents were mortgaged. Time and again it seemed as if all would be lost. More than once Watt and Boulton felt that this might be a blessing. The mine owners, for instance, refused to pay for the engines which had saved them thousands of dollars. Dishonest persons stole and used their patents. They were continually annoyed by rumors that a better engine was on the point of being completed. Efforts were even made to get Parliament to take away their patents.

"We are in the same state as the old Roman," Watt wrote, "who was found guilty of raising better crops than his neighbors, and was ordered to bring before the assembly of the people his farming instruments for inspection. He complied, and when he was able to speak, said, 'These, O Romans, are the instruments of our art, but I cannot bring into our meeting the labors, the sweats, the watchings, the anxieties, the cares which produce the crops.' So everyone sees the reward which we may yet probably receive from our labors; but few consider the price we have paid for that reward, which is by no means certain."

Difficulty after difficulty was, however, battled down. Parliament refused to take away the patents. Persons who used them without right were punished. The mine owners were forced to pay what they owed. The business, after long waiting and untold distress, began to prosper.

Old Age at Hearthfield

The partnership between Watt and Boulton came to an end in 1800. Watt was now quite rich. Relieved of business cares and worry, his health improved. He built a beautiful country home at Hearthfield. From there he made trips to different parts of Scotland, Wales, and England. To Hearthfield came old friends and the greatest men of England to visit him. Inventing continued to give him the greatest pleasure. A room was built up in the attic of his house, and there he would work for days at a time. This room remains just as it was in 1819, because Mr. Watt's home was preserved as a museum.

James Watt spent a great deal of his life making improvements in engines of various kinds. His tireless efforts proved to the world that machines could give human beings great power and prosperity.

Even today, people in Europe and America commonly honor the memory of this great inventor by refering to a unit of electric power as a "Watt." If you buy a light bulb in the United States, it will normally be stamped with the amount of light it will give off, for example, "60 Watts". This is one small way that Americans have chosen to honor the memory of this gifted inventor.

WATT'S WORKROOM AT HEARTHFIELD

Comprehension Questions

1. What was the chief means of power used in the production of food and shelter during the 1700s?
2. What was James Watt's most significant invention?
3. Who or what was Beelzebub?
4. How did people make use of the steam engine during the time that Watt lived?
5. What type of problems did Watt and Boulton have when they tried to sell their new steam engine?
6. What tribute or honor was given to Mr. Watt in the United States?

ROBERT FULTON

Chapter 2

Robert Fulton and the Invention of the Steamboat

On August 17, 1807, a curious crowd of people in New York gathered at a boat landing. Tied to the dock was a strange-looking craft. A smokestack rose above the deck. Large paddle wheels were attached to the sides of the boat. Suddenly, the clouds of smoke from the smokestack grew larger, the paddle wheels turned, and the boat, to the astonishment of all, moved. It was "Fulton's Folly," the *Clermont*, on her first trip to the city of Albany.

The First Boats

The first boat used by man was probably the trunk of a fallen tree, moved about by a broken branch or pole. Then some person saw that a better boat could be made by tying several logs together to make a raft. But rafts are hard to control, so the heart of a log was hollowed out by a stone ax or fire, to make a still better boat, or strips of birch bark were skillfully fastened together to form a graceful canoe. Boats were constructed also of rough-hewn boards. With such primitive craft, voyages of hundreds of miles were made up and down great rivers like the Mississippi, or along the shores of inland seas like the Great Lakes.

The ancient Phoenicians were the first great sailors. Their boats, called galleys, were sometimes two to three hundred feet long. These were of two kinds, merchantmen and war vessels. The merchantmen were propelled partly by sails and partly by oars, but on the war vessels, when in battle, oars only were used. On a single boat there were often several hundred oarsmen or galley slaves. These galley slaves were usually prisoners of war. They were chained to the oar benches, and to force them to row, they were often beaten within an inch

A MEDIEVAL GALLEY

of their lives. In enormous sail-and-oar vessels the Phoenicians, around 900 B.C., crossed the Mediterranean in every direction, pushed out into the Atlantic Ocean, and went as far north as England.

The main improvement in boat making, from the time of the Phoenicians until the first trip of the *Clermont*, was to do away with oars and to use sails only.

It was not until about fifty years before the time of Columbus that oars were generally discarded and large boats were propelled entirely by sails. Sailboats were, to be sure, a great improvement over oar boats. Yet at best they were slow and unreliable, held back alike by calm and storm. The Pilgrims were ten weeks in crossing the Atlantic, and in the time of George Washington, the regular trip required six weeks.

The First Steamboat

The first American to attempt the propelling of a boat by steam was William Henry, a gunsmith from Lancaster, Pennsylvania. In 1760 Mr. Henry was in England on business. He took great interest in the talk going on then about the use of steam to drive machinery, propel boats, and the like. On his return to America, he built an engine fashioned after one of Newcomen's engines, and placed it in a boat with paddles. The boat did not go well, and a little later was accidentally sunk. Though unsuccessful, Henry never lost his interest in steamboats.

The first American to propel a boat by steam successfully was John Fitch. Fitch was a frequent visitor at the home of Henry, and probably got the idea of building a steamboat from him. However that may be, Fitch built a better boat than Henry, and he is regarded by some people as the real inventor of the steamboat.

TRIAL TRIP OF FITCH'S STEAMBOAT

Fitch built his first boat in 1787. The engine was made in America, but was copied from the one built by Watt. Along each side of the boat stood two sets of three paddles. To move the boat, these were given a motion like the stroke in paddling a canoe. Six paddles entered the water, while six came out. Fitch had great difficulty in obtaining the money to build the boat, and even after it was built, the boiler had to be made larger. Finally, after much delay and anxiety, all was ready for a public trial. This took place at Philadelphia. Men like Washington, Jefferson, and Franklin came to see the new wonder. It was interesting to see a boat propelled by steam, but there was no great enthusiasm because its speed was only three or four miles an hour.

The next year Fitch built a second boat, with the paddles placed at the stern. But the boat could not be made to go faster than a man could walk, and it was no more of a success than the first. Fitch succeeded, however, in 1790, in making a boat sixty feet long and eight feet wide with paddles at the stern, which had a speed of seven miles an hour. After a trial at Philadelphia, it made regular trips between Philadelphia and Trenton for the rest of the summer. Fitch's boat ran between two and three thousand miles with no serious accident, but it cost more to run the boat than the fares amounted to, so the venture failed.

Fitch found his way to New York, and worked on developing a screw steamboat there in 1796. He had long since spent all his money. Nobody would help him, and therefore the screw steamboat had to be given up. Completely discouraged, Fitch retired to a farm in Kentucky. He believed in the steamboat until the last. He was confident that the day would come when steamboats would be running on all our large rivers and across the ocean. "The day will come," he said, "when some more powerful man will get fame and riches from my invention; but now no one will believe that poor John Fitch can do anything worthy of attention."

Driving along the shore of the Delaware one day, John Stevens of New Jersey saw Fitch's little steamboat puffing slowly along between Philadelphia and Trenton. He followed it to the next landing and examined it with care. He had long been interested in steamboats and now decided to build one. He set to work with great energy, and by his enthusiasm he induced Robert R. Livingston of New York to share in the enterprise. After almost ten years of planning and experimenting, these men thought they were at the point of success. The boat of which they expected so much was launched in 1798. But alas! It could run only three miles an hour in still water, and was soon given up as a failure.

Stevens, undaunted, continued his experiments year after year. Model after model was made. Some of these boats had paddle wheels extending from the sides; some were propelled by a single revolving screw at the stern, and others had two screws. Stevens experimented also with different kinds of boilers. He was so successful that he came very near winning the prize that was afterward awarded to Robert Fulton. The very next month after Fulton's first boat made its trial trip, Stevens launched the *Phoenix*, which was as good a boat as the *Clermont*. His screw propeller, as well as his boilers, were later used extensively on ocean steamships. Thus, after Fulton, Stevens did more than any other man to make the steamboat a practical success.

Inventors in England were also busy, and the most successful of these was William Symington. Funds to build the trial boat were supplied by Lord Dundas, who hoped that steam might replace horses in towing canal barges. The *Charlotte Dundas*, Symington's boat, was ready for trial in 1802.

She was a stern-wheeler, that is, she was propelled by a paddle wheel at the stern. An engine built by Boulton and Watt supplied the power. The new boat took two barges of seventy tons burden each, and in the face of a strong wind towed them down the canal twenty miles in six hours.

Lord Dundas was delighted. He wanted this way of towing adopted. The other owners of the canal were not convinced, however, that there would be much saved by the change. They also feared that the new boat would damage the banks of the canal. Lord Dundas finally succeeded in interesting the Duke of Bridgewater, who gave Symington an order for eight boats like the *Charlotte Dundas*. Had these been built, Symington would today probably be known as the inventor of the steamboat. Unfortunately, the Duke died about this time, and the boats were never built. The *Charlotte Dundas*

was anchored in a side creek to rot, and Symington gave up the project in despair.

Though men had been working and experimenting for many years, a practical steamboat, that is, one that could be used at a good profit to its owners, was yet to be built. There was great need for such a steamboat, and Watt's engine was strong enough to propel it. But no one seemed able to build a boat of the right shape, to make the right kind of propeller, or to harness Watt's engine to it in the right way. So many attempts had been made, and there had been so many failures, that most men came to believe it was impossible to make a successful steamboat. The man who first succeeded in doing the "impossible" was Robert Fulton.

Fulton's Early Life

Robert Fulton was born at Little Britain, Lancaster County, Pennsylvania, in 1765. His father, though not successful in money matters, was highly respected; he was a leader in the Presbyterian Church, and held several minor public offices of honor. His mother was an excellent woman who had more education than most women of the time. She taught Robert reading, writing, and arithmetic until he was eight years of age.

Robert was then sent to school, where he acquired a good elementary education. He was not a superior scholar. Books interested him much less than painting or the shop of the gunsmith. Nobody knows who taught him to paint, unless it was Major Andre, who was later hanged as a spy. Major Andre lived for some months at Lancaster and gave painting lessons there. It is possible that Robert was one of his pupils. At any rate, the boy learned, when young, to draw and to paint.

He had some talent, and perhaps was inspired to become an artist by the example of Benjamin West, one of America's greatest painters during this period. Mr. West was often in Lancaster when he was young, and he painted a portrait of Robert's father and mother. Mr. Henry, of whom mention has already been made, had many of Mr. West's pictures and Robert used to go to his home to look at them. It may be true that Mr. Henry talked to Robert about his steamboat on these visits. They may have talked about how fine it would be to invent one. Perhaps this led Fulton to give up art and become an engineer and inventor.

Besides being fond of drawing and painting, Robert was interested in tools. Not far from his home, there were shops where muskets were made for the soldiers of the Revolutionary War. Robert was a frequent visitor there, and he spent much time in making drawings of guns and tinkering with broken muskets.

His ability to make things showed itself early. One day, Robert was very late to school. "Robert, why are you so late?" asked the teacher.

"I was making a pencil out of a piece of lead," he replied.

The teacher looked at the pencil and thought it was a good one. In just a few days, all the children had lead pencils.

At the age of seventeen, Fulton left Lancaster and went to Philadelphia. He gave his attention principally to painting portraits and miniatures, but he turned his hand to anything that came along. He drew plans for machinery and for carriages, and even houses. In this way he not only made his own living, but by the time he was twenty-one, he already had saved forty thousand dollars.

While living in Philadelphia, Fulton became acquainted with Benjamin Franklin. Knowing that Fulton would never succeed as an artist unless he prepared himself better, Franklin advised him to go to London to study.

FULTON AND THE LEAD PENCIL

Fulton decided to do this; but just then his father died, leaving his mother without a home. He therefore took a part of the forty thousand dollars that he had planned to spend on his art education, and bought his mother a farm, where she lived in contentment and plenty for many years.

Studying Art in London

With a letter from Franklin to Benjamin West, Fulton set out for London, where he landed early in 1787. He had about two thousand dollars in his pocket. Not a large sum with which to get an education; but lack of money has never stopped young men of character and energy. Benjamin West received the young man with kindness, and besides giving him instruction, helped him in other ways.

The story of Fulton's life then is told in a letter to his mother. "I had an art to learn by which I was to earn my bread, but little to support me while I was doing it. Many, many a silent, solitary hour have I spent in most anxious study, pondering how to make funds to support me until the fruits of my labor should be sufficient. . . . Thus I went on for nearly four years — kindly cared for by all who knew me, or I had long before now been crushed by poverty's cold wind and freezing rain. When last summer I was invited by Lord Courtney down to his

FULTON MEETS LORD COURTNEY'S FRIENDS

country seat to paint a picture of him, ... His Lordship was so much pleased that he introduced me to all his friends. It is just now that I am beginning to get a little money and pay some debts that I was obliged to contract. So I hope in about six months to be clear with the world, or in other words out of debt, and then start fair to make all I can."

Engineer and Inventor

After four years of study, Fulton felt that he was ready to take up his life work. Among the friends to whom Lord Courtney introduced him was the Duke of Bridgewater, who became one of Fulton's good friends. Whether it was the talks about steamboats and canals with the Duke of Bridgewater, or whether it was his talent for mechanics and invention grown strong, we do not know, but Fulton suddenly gave up the idea of being an artist and decided to become an engineer.

Whether Fulton would have become a great artist or not, no one can tell. He surely had artistic ability. He had been taught by the best teachers of England, and had gained some recognition and honor as an artist. In any event, if the world lost a great artist, it gained a great inventor. Nor was his training as an artist entirely lost when he turned engineer. He was able to make his ideas clear by means of drawings, and was also able to draw his own plans and designs. A successful person often needs to have many skills.

Immediately after making his decision, Fulton went to Birmingham, England, where he lived for two years. There he studied the great canals that were being built. He became acquainted with Watt and his engines, and saw the best mechanics in Europe at work. His active mind soon began to turn out invention after invention. He invented a double inclined plane for raising and lowering canal boats from one level to the other, a machine for spinning hemp, and one for twisting hemp rope.

A project to which he gave much time was his submarine or plunging boat. Fulton could go down into the water in this diving boat twenty feet or more, and move about. In this way he could get near a vessel without being seen, and then by means of a cigar-shaped torpedo that he invented could blow it up. In an experiment at Brest, France, in 1805, he accomplished this. Fulton thought his diving boat and torpedoes would make war vessels useless, and would do away with war on the seas. He tried in turn to get the French and English governments to adopt this invention; he also offered it to the United States. Nothing, however, came of his efforts. Submarine and torpedo boats have since come into general use, but they have not abolished naval war, as Fulton hoped they would.

Experimenting With Steamboats

We do not know when Fulton first began to think of making a steamboat. But we have his own words for saying that in 1802 he began "experiments with a view to discover the principles on which boats or vessels should be propelled through the water by the power of steam engines." Fulton did not undertake to make a successful steamboat without awareness of the failures of Fitch, Stevens, Symington, and others, without understanding that after so many failures, men who still thought a practical steamboat could be built were looked upon as madmen. Yet it has ever been so. The men who win fame and fortune do what other people say cannot be done. Fulton learned all he could from the mistakes and failures of others. To make sure that he was right before he went ahead, he did what was still more important, he made experiment after experiment.

He built a model boat, four feet long and twelve inches wide, provided with two strong clock springs for power. Experiments were made with propellers that opened and shut like a duck's foot, with side paddle wheels, stern paddle wheels, side oars, screws, and paddles fastened to an endless chain passing over two wheels. Fulton was convinced that side paddle wheels were the best. He

FULTON SHOWING HIS BOAT TO LIVINGSTON, IN PARIS

learned also that the propelling surface of the different paddles combined should be twice the exposed surface of the bow. In addition, he worked out a table to show the power that was needed to move boats of different sizes at different speeds. With this information, Fulton was ready to experiment on a larger scale. He began to dream of boats that would make the trip between New York City and Albany in twelve hours.

Robert R. Livingston was at this time the United States' minister to France. Fulton, then living in France, succeeded in getting him to advance the money to make the larger experiment. The two formed an agreement that if the experiment proved successful, they would construct and run steamboats between New York City and Albany. To protect themselves in their invention, Livingston secured from the State of New York, in the name of himself and Fulton, the exclusive right for twenty years to navigate steamboats on all the waters of the state. No one thought, even in 1803, that there was any danger that such an invention would be a success.

Fulton finally began to work on a boat seventy feet long, eight feet wide, and with a three foot draft. The paddle wheels were twelve feet in diameter, and the engine was about eight horse power. When the boat was nearly ready for the trial trip, a violent storm arose one night, and so beat the boat about that it broke in two and sank to the bottom of the Seine. Fulton was awakened from an anxious sleep by the shouts of his servant, who exclaimed, "Oh, sir! The boat has broken to pieces and has gone to the bottom."

Fulton hurried to the river to find that this was all too true. He labored for twenty-four hours without stopping, to raise the boat. The machinery was little harmed, but the hull was such a wreck that it had to be entirely rebuilt. This occupied several months, and the boat was not again ready for trial until August 1803.

The trial trip was thus described in one of the French newspapers: "At six o'clock in the evening, aided by only three persons, he (Fulton) put his boat in motion . . . and for an hour and a half he produced the curious spectacle of a boat moved by wheels, . . . these wheels being provided with paddles or flat plates, and moved by a fire engine. In following it along the wharf, the speed against the current of the Seine was about that of a rapid walker, that is, about four miles an hour. . . It was maneuvered with ease, turning to the right and left, came to anchor and started again." Not only was the new boat declared a success by the French newspapers, but the success was such as to lead Livingston and Fulton to begin the building of a boat for actual service on the Hudson river.

FIRST TRIP OF THE CLERMONT

Building the Clermont

In August 1803 a twenty-four horsepower engine was ordered from Boulton and Watt, to be shipped to New York. Boulton and Watt at first refused the order, because the British government would not let them ship the engine. The government probably feared that the engine was to be used in a torpedo boat by the French. After much delay, permission was secured, and the order was accepted. Fulton, who was then in England, went to Birmingham to see that the engine was built just as he wanted it. He was right in feeling that the success of his boat depended upon how the engine worked. Fulton arrived at New York in December 1806. He at once hired a famous shipbuilder, whose yards were on the East River, to build the hull of the boat. The boat was to be one hundred and fifty feet long, thirteen feet wide, and was to draw two feet of water.

When it became known that the new boat was to be a steamboat, idle crowds would collect around, and talk about the project as "Fulton's Folly." Nor did these crowds take kindly to the idea of a steamboat; they even went so far as to try to destroy it. Neither did the owners of the sailboats on the East River like the idea, so when they were passing by in their sloops they would bump into the *Clermont*. It became necessary for Fulton to hire watchmen to protect the boat both day and night.

No one had any faith in the success of the venture. When, in 1806, Livingston and Fulton offered to take Stevens into partnership with them, he refused, and said, "Mr. Fulton's plan can never succeed."

At another time, when it became necessary to raise a thousand dollars to complete work on the *Clermont*, Fulton went to some of his friends for aid. Most of them told him they were too wise to sink good money in such a wild scheme. After much difficulty,

AN OLD FERRYBOAT TICKET

however, Fulton succeeded in obtaining the needed money, but only by promising his friends to keep their names secret. They feared that they would be ridiculed for their folly.

The *Clermont*, when completed, was a strange-looking craft. There was a mast at each end, but these carried very small sails. A little to the front of the center stood the smokestack and the working beam and piston.

Projecting from the center over each side was a great uncovered paddle wheel. "She looked," said one observer, "like a backwoods sawmill mounted on a scow and set on fire."

First Trip of the Clermont

The *Clermont* was ready for her first trip up the Hudson River on August 17, 1807. Here is Fulton's own story of the trip:

"The moment arrived at which the word was to be given for the boat to move. My friends were in groups on the deck. There was anxiety mixed with fear among them.

They were silent, sad, and weary. I read in their looks nothing but disaster, and almost repented of my efforts. The signal was given, and the boat moved on a short distance and then stopped. . . . To the silence of the preceding moment, now succeeded murmurs of discontent, agitation, whispers, and shrugs. I could hear distinctly repeated, 'I told you it was so; it is a foolish scheme; I wish we were well out of it.'

"I elevated myself on a platform; I stated I knew not what the matter was, but if they would be quiet and give me half an hour, I would either go on or abandon the voyage for that time. . . . I went below and found . . . the cause. . . . In a short time it was fixed. The boat was again put in motion. She continued to move on. All were still incredulous. None seemed willing to trust the evidence of their senses. We left the fair city of New York; we passed through the romantic and evervarying scenery of the Highlands; we admired the clustering houses of Albany; we reached its shores — and then, even then, when all seemed achieved, I was the victim of disappointment.

"It was then doubted if it could be done again, or if done, it was doubted if it could be made of any great value."

In another letter Fulton wrote:

"My steamboat voyage to Albany and back has turned out more favorably than I had calculated. The distance from New York city to Albany is one hundred and fifty miles. I ran it up in thirty-two hours and down in thirty. I had a light breeze against me the whole way, both going and coming, and the voyage has been performed wholly by the power of the steam engine. I overtook many sloops and schooners beating to the windward, and parted with them as if they had been at anchor.

"The power of propelling boats by steam is now fully proved. The morning I left New York there were not perhaps thirty people in the city, who believed that the boat would ever move one mile an hour, or be of the least utility, and while we were putting off from the wharf, I heard many sarcastic remarks . . .

"Having employed much time, money, and zeal in accomplishing this work, it gives me, as it will you, great pleasure to see it fully answers my expectations. It will give a cheap and quick conveyance to the merchandise on the Mississippi, Missouri, and other great rivers, which are now laying open their treasures to our countrymen; and although the prospect of personal gain has been some inducement to me, yet I feel . . . more pleasure in reflecting on the immense advantage that my country will derive from the invention."

The passage of the *Clermont* caused great excitement among the people along the way. Here is a description written by one who stood on the bank and saw the boat go by:

"It was in the early autumn of the year 1807, that a group of villagers was gathered on a high bluff just opposite Poughkeepsie, on the west bank of the Hudson, attracted by the appearance of a strange, dark-looking craft that was slowly making its way up the river. Some imagined it to be a sea monster, whilst others did not hesitate to express their belief that it was a sign of the approaching judgment. . . . The dense clouds of smoke, as they rose, wave upon wave, added still more to the wonderment of the rustics.

"On her return trip, the curiosity she excited was scarcely less intense — the whole country talked of nothing but the sea monster, belching forth fire and smoke. The fishermen became terrified and rowed homeward, and they saw nothing but destruction devastating their fishing grounds; whilst the wreaths of black vapor and rushing noise of the paddle wheels, foaming with the stirred-up waters, produced great excitement amongst the boatmen."

On her return from Albany, the *Clermont* was put in dock. The paddle wheels were covered, decks were made over the boilers, the rudder was repaired, and three cabins of twelve berths each were fitted up to accommodate forty to fifty passengers. Thus equipped, the *Clermont* started in September 1807 to make regular trips between Albany and New York, and continued to do so until the Hudson river froze over late in November. As a passenger vessel, she was a success from the first. To be sure, people were in great fear that the boiler would burst, or that the boat would catch on fire. There was also a vague feeling that something terrible must surely happen to the "monster that defied storm and tide and belched forth fire and smoke."

The fare was just the same as that on the sailboats, three dollars. But it took sailboats, on the average, forty-eight hours to make the trip. The average time of the *Clermont* was only thirty-six hours. It was not long before she was crowded with passengers.

Steamboats on Rivers and Ocean

Most great inventions are a long time in coming, but after their usefulness is shown they are quickly adopted. This was true of the steamboat. During the winter of 1807 the *Clermont* was made better and larger, and renamed the *North River*. So great was the demand that within the next eight years, Fulton constructed, or allowed to be built according to his plans, no fewer than ten other boats for service on the Hudson River, Long Island Sound, and the Potomac. Fulton also designed and built great steam ferryboats to cross the East River and the Hudson River. Steven's *Phoenix* began in 1807 to make regular trips on

WATCHING THE CLERMONT STEAM UP THE HUDSON RIVER

the Delaware river. By 1810 steamboats could be seen trailing long lines of smoke up and down the Mississippi and the Ohio. They were also introduced into England and Russia, and even into far-away India.

Fulton's belief in the commercial usefulness of steamboats was so great that he not only expected them to be placed on all the rivers of the civilized world, but he hoped to see them on the great oceans also.

The first steam vessel to cross the Atlantic Ocean was the *Savannah*, in 1819. Fulton did not live to witness this great event, for he died in 1815. To a great idea, steam navigation — he had given freely of his time, his talents, and his money. Others like Fitch helped him to succeed. Men like Stevens improved on his invention. Together they gave to the world a more successful means of travel, transportation, and communication. Yet to Robert Fulton belongs the honor of being the first inventor to make a genuinely successful steamboat.

Comprehension Questions

1. What name did the Phoenicians give to their ships?
2. Who was John Fitch?
3. Where was Robert Fulton born?
4. Who was Benjamin West?
5. What nickname did the people give to Fulton's first successful steamboat?

Chapter 3

George Stephenson and the Invention of the Locomotive

With Watt's steam engine to pump out the water and to hoist the coal, miners were going deeper into the earth, and were bringing out more coal than ever before. The "new giant" turned countless mills for grinding corn and wheat, and was harnessed to the machines of the 1800's for spinning and weaving cotton and wool. The day of cheap fuel, food, and clothing seemed very near. Only one thing was lacking: a cheap overland transportation system to take raw materials like fuel, wheat, cotton, and wool to mills and factories and then carry the finished products to market. There was great need of a locomotive that would do good work at a small

GEORGE STEPHENSON

cost. Men began to work on such a locomotive. They did not, of course, try to invent a new engine, but to modify Watt's stationary engine into a serviceable moving engine. George Stephenson succeeded in doing this.

His Parents and Home

About eight miles west of Newcastle, England, is the mining village of Wylam. Near the east end of the town there stands a two-story house with four rooms. The lower west room was once the home of the Stephenson family. The floor of this single room, which served alike for kitchen, dining room, parlor, and sleeping room, was of clay. The walls were unplastered, and the rafters were bare. Here, on June 9, 1781, George Stephenson was born.

The father was the fireman of the Newcomen engine at the Wylam mine. With a wage of not more than a dollar and a half per week, and with six children in the family, there was scarcely enough for food and little to spare for clothing. The family was so poor that none of the children were sent to school. But George received from his father and mother traits of character and practical learning skills that were even better than riches, and more than made up for his lack of formal education. It was a trait of his to have definite ambitions. He made his plans and then advanced one step at a time. When the desired position was secured, he was not satisfied, but prepared himself for a further advance.

Upward Step By Step

When George was old enough, he was put to work. His first job was herding cows, at four cents a day.

Growing older and stronger, he was hired out to do light farm work. He drove horses, milked cows, and hoed in the garden. Later he joined his brother James at the mine, as a "picker" to clean the coal off dirt and stones. His wages were now twelve cents a day, and increased to sixteen cents when he became driver of the gin horse.

Driving a gin horse was a fairly good job, but George wanted to be an engineer. To be assistant fireman was the first step. Great was his joy when, at fourteen, he was made assistant to his father, at the wage of twenty-five cents a day.

By age fifteen George had become a fireman, and was still ambitious to be an engineer. He spent the greater part of his spare time in studying his engine and in learning how each part worked. It was a great event in his life when some two years later his wages were raised to three dollars a week. "I am now" he was heard to remark, "set with money for life."

Not long after this, a new mine was opened, and George became the engineer. It was his duty to run the engine, keep it in order, and look after the pumps. If for any reason the engine stopped, and he was unable to make it go, he was to call upon the chief engineer of the mine. But the youth knew every part of his engine so well that he never needed to call for help.

STEPHENSON MODELING AN ENGINE IN CLAY

Modeling engines in clay was his main pastime. He made models of those that he had seen, and of others that were described to him. In this way he first heard of the engines of Boulton and Watt. Wanting to know more about them, he was told that he would find them described in books. Alas! George could not read. He did not even know his letters. He now realized that to advance further, he must be able to get information from books. Although he was as large as a grown man, and was doing a man's work, he decided that he must go to night school.

He went to school three nights a week, taking lessons in reading, spelling, and writing. During one or two winters, he took lessons also in arithmetic. This was easy for him. The secret was his perseverance. He spent his spare time about the mine on his "sums." The problems solved during the day, he carried to his teacher in the evening, and received new "sums" for the following day.

About this time, he decided to learn braking. A brakeman operates the machinery that hoists the coal. The work is responsible and well paid. A good friend allowed George to try his hand at the work, and although only twenty years of age, he was soon braking at another mine.

Thus, through attention to work and study, and through perseverance, George Stephenson advanced step by step from herdboy to brakeman; he educated himself, and became a skilled worker.

Further Improvement

To add to his income, Stephenson began mending and making shoes in the evening. Among the shoes sent to him was a pair belonging to the girl who became his wife, a young woman of sweet temper, kind disposition, and good common sense.

Happy in his work and content in his home, Stephenson began to make better use of his spare hours in the evening. He studied mechanics, and came to know thoroughly the engines of both Newcomen and Watt. He also began to model machines. One of these was a perpetual-motion machine. Though it proved a failure, as all others have, it gave him opportunity to stretch his powers of invention.

Shortly after the death of his wife in 1806, Stephenson went to Scotland to superintend a Boulton and Watt engine in a cotton factory. This gave him the chance he had long wanted, to work with one of those wonderful machines. He remained there a year, returning with more than a hundred dollars saved from his wages.

Meanwhile his father had been injured in an accident. While he was inside a Newcomen engine, a workman turned on the steam. The blast struck him full in the face, not only scalding him terribly, but putting out his eyes. The poor man struggled along against poverty as best he could. After the son's return, his first step was to pay his father's debts. A little later he moved his parents to Killingworth, where they lived for many years, supported entirely by him.

An Engine Doctor

For some unknown reason, the engine at the High Pit, a coal mine near Killingworth, didn't work, and the miners were driven out by the water. The local engineers were called in, but each in turn didn't discover the trouble. One day Stephenson went over to the mine and examined the engine carefully. "Well, George," asked a miner, "what do you make o' her? Do you think you could do anything to improve her?"

"I could alter her," he replied, "and make her draw. In a week's time I could send you back to the bottom."

This conversation was reported to the manager, who in desperation decided to give Stephenson a chance.

"George," said the manager, "they tell me that you think you can repair the engine at High Pit."

"Yes, sir, I think I could."

"If that's the case, I'll give you a fair trial. The engineers around here are all beat; and if you do what they cannot do, you may depend upon it, I will make you a happy man for life."

The engine was taken apart, and many changes were made. These were completed in about three days, and the engine began pumping. By ten o'clock that night the water was lower in the pit than it had been for a long time. By the end of the week the workmen were "sent back to the bottom." Stephenson had made good his word.

His skill as an engine doctor was spread abroad. He was called upon to prescribe remedies for all the wheezy, creaky, pumping engines of the neighborhood. As an engine doctor his wages were good, and he soon left the "regular" workmen behind. They in turn were jealous of him and looked upon him as a "quack." The manager of the High Pit, however, believed in him, and succeeded in 1812 in making him engine wright at Killingworth.

GEORGE STEPHENSON AND HIS SON ROBERT STUDYING TOGETHER

Educating His Son

Stephenson often thought of the difficulties he had in life because he lacked a thorough education. He was determined to give his only son Robert, born in 1803, a good education. When Robert was old enough he was sent to a local private school. The education to be had there scarcely went beyond the primer and writing, and it soon seemed best to send Robert to a private Christian school at Newcastle. This was expensive, and Stephenson's earnings were small. Besides, he was the sole support of his afflicted parents. How was the money to be obtained? "I betook myself," said Stephenson long afterward, "to mending my neighbors' clocks and watches at night, after my daily labor was done, and thus I obtained the means of educating my son."

Robert went to and from Newcastle on a donkey. But it was not only Robert who was at school at Newcastle, his father shared his schooling. Their evenings were spent together in going over the lessons of the next day. Books were brought from the library to be read. When the desired books could not be taken out, Robert would bring home descriptions and sketches for his father's information. The son thus helped to educate the father — but such a father! Do you wonder that Robert was later proud of saying that if his success had been great, it was mainly to the example and training of his father that he owed it? Many parents living today fail to understand how important it is for children to see that learning is a life-long process.

The First Railroads and Locomotives

Stephenson as engine wright at Killingworth not only had to keep the pumping and hoisting engines repaired; it was also his duty to look after all the other machinery. As he traveled from mine to mine, he was on the lookout for any improvements. This led him to start thinking about locomotives.

George Stephenson and the Invention of the Locomotive

The locomotive was still looked upon as a curious and expensive toy. Stephenson saw more clearly than most others of what great use it might be, not only in carrying coal to market, but in transporting all kinds of products. He turned all his knowledge of machinery, and all the power of his inventive mind, to the making of a locomotive.

There are three parts to a railroad: the locomotive, the cars, and the track on which these run. The first railways were tramways, used to haul coal from the mines to the wharves, where it was loaded on boats to be carried to distant cities. Such tramways were often ten to twelve miles long. They were constructed by building a roadway almost level, and by placing, upon wooden crossties, two wooden rails. At some mines, a thin plate of iron was nailed on the upper surface of the rails. Cast-iron rails, three or four feet long, were also common.

The cars had a large, hopper-like, wooden body. This huge body rested on a wooden platform made of heavy wooden beams. These were fastened at each end to an iron axle, which connected the two supporting cast-iron wheels. A horse could pull, at the rate of two or three miles an hour, two or more of these cars, loaded altogether with from eight to ten tons of coal.

Two parts of a railroad, the rail tramway and the cars, were already in place when Stephenson began to make a locomotive. His object was to invent an engine that would replace horses on the tramways. Therefore, if his locomotive was to be successful it must do the same work, not only more satisfactorily, but at less cost than it could be done by horses.

The idea of such a locomotive did not originate with Stephenson, nor was he the first to make one. That honor belongs to Richard Trevithick, who built a locomotive as early as 1804. This locomotive could haul ten tons, along with the cars, men, fuel, and the like, at the rate of five or six miles an hour. For a short time it was in successful use. But it broke so many of the small cast-iron rails of which the road was made, and ran off the track so often, that it was soon put aside and the engine degraded to working a pump. The trouble was with the track and not with the engine. With a little more perseverance, Trevithick might have succeeded in making a successful locomotive and have risen to fame and fortune. But Trevithick was a genius, fond of trying new projects. He left his locomotive, after a few trial trips, to take care of itself, and thought no more about it.

No one devoted much attention to the locomotive for some time. Still, the idea was not lost. In 1811, Mr.

Blenkinsop, a mine manager near Leeds, England, decided to build one. Blenkinsop followed Trevithick's design. The new features of this locomotive were the two cylinders and a toothed wheel that was designed to grip the metal rails firmly.

This toothed wheel was designed to overcome an imaginary difficulty. Even the wisest men of the time thought that if a load were placed behind an engine, the "grip" or "bite" of its smooth wheels on the smooth rails would be so slight that the wheels of the engine would spin round and round in the same place and the engine would never move. Naturally, Blenkinsop thought that the toothed wheel working in a rack rail was necessary, if his engine was to draw a load.

Blenkinsop's locomotive, when loaded lightly, traveled at the rate of ten miles an hour. It would draw ninety tons at three and a half miles an hour on a dead level, or fifteen tons up hill. The locomotive cost two thousand dollars, and did the work of sixteen horses. For more than twenty years it was in constant use, and was the first successful locomotive ever made.

Encouraged by Blenkinsop's success, Mr. Blackett, of Wylam, resolved to try a locomotive at his mine. The first one made for him "flew all to pieces" on first trial.

He had a second one built, which like the first was modeled after Trevithick's and Blenkinsop's engines. The

PUFFING BILLY

new locomotive had a flywheel, and the driving wheel was cogged and traveled in a rack rail. This engine could haul eight or nine loaded cars at the rate of a mile an hour. It was too heavy for the track, and the rails were always breaking. The driver was asked one day how he got on. "Get on?" he asked. "We don't get on; we only get off!"

The chief cause of the failure was the cogged driving wheel working in the rack rail. Blackett learned by experiment that these were unnecessary. His third locomotive, built in 1813, was fitted with smooth wheels. This new engine, *Puffing Billy*, was more successful. It was easy to manage, and pulled ten to fourteen loaded cars, having a combined weight of twenty tons, at the rate of four or five miles an hour.

Stephenson's First Locomotive

Stephenson's first engine, *Blucher*, was built in 1814. It was not much of a success. The best that *Blucher* could do was to pull thirty tons on a grade, at the rate of four miles an hour. After a year's trial, it was found that it cost just as much to haul coal by steam power as by horse power. There was little encouragement in this, for the success of the locomotive depended on its economy.

Stephenson began to work with new vigor, and early in 1815 completed a second engine. This new engine had a wrought-iron boiler eight feet long and thirty-four inches wide, with a single flue twenty inches in diameter. The flue was furnished with a steam blast. The steam blast, or forced draft, was one of Stephenson's wonderful inventions. In the earlier locomotives, the steam after doing its work in the cylinder was allowed to escape into the air with a horrible hissing that terrified both man and beast. Stephenson noticed that the steam escaped at much greater speed from the cylinder than the smoke came from the smokestack. It occurred to him that if this escaping steam were directed into the smokestack, it would produce a draft. This would increase the intensity of the fire, making it possible with the same size boiler to produce a greater amount of steam. The experiment was no sooner tried than the speed and the power of the engine were more than doubled. It is not too much to say that, without the forced draft and the later invention of a boiler with many small tubes connecting the fire box and the smokestack, locomotives of that period would have continued to drag along at a rate of not more than four or five miles an hour.

A Successful Locomotive

In Stephenson's first engine, the power was applied to the driving wheels by means of cogwheels. Stephenson saw that if the locomotive was to be a success, the power would have to be applied directly. In the new engine, the two cylinders were connected directly with the four driving wheels. To obtain the necessary freedom of motion, and to avoid the friction and jars due to rough places in the track, ball-and-socket joints were used to join the connecting rods with the crossheads of the cylinders, and with the crank pins of the driving wheels. Stephenson planned also to connect each pair of driving wheels by bars fastened to cranks in each axle. Workmen were, however, not able at this time to forge these cranks, and it was necessary, for the time being, to use connecting chains.

Stephenson thus succeeded in making an engine having direct connection between the cylinders and the driving wheels, direct connection between all the wheels, and a forced draft. These are the essential points in all the engines that have been built since. Stephenson therefore did for the locomotive what Watt had done for the steam engine.

Building the First Steam Railroad

Although Stephenson's locomotives were in daily use at Killingworth, and had been for years, nobody paid much attention to them except mine owners. There seemed little prospect that the locomotive would come into general use. Stephenson, however, had a growing faith in his invention.

In 1821 Mr. Edward Pease obtained from Parliament authority to construct a tramway between Stockton and Darlington. Not many days later, a stranger called on Mr. Pease, describing himself as "only the engine wright at Killingworth." George Stephenson wished to be the engineer of the new road. Mr. Pease saw that he was the very man for the job.

When the Stockton and Darlington Railroad was planned, there was no thought of using locomotives on it. None of the directors had any faith in them. Stationary engines were to be put at the very steepest grades, but the bulk of

STEPHENSON ON THE ENGINE LOCOMOTION, AT THE OPENING OF THE STOCKTON AND DARLINGTON RAILROAD

the hauling was to be done by horses. Stephenson lost no chance to tell Mr. Pease of his locomotives. "One locomotive is worth fifty horses. Come over to Killingworth and see what my engines can do; seeing is believing." Mr. Pease finally went to Killingworth and with him seeing was believing. Three of Stephenson's locomotives were ordered to be ready for the opening of the railroad line.

As the time for opening the road came near, Stephenson became anxious. He was hopeful, however. At dinner with his son Robert one evening, he said: "I venture to tell you that I think you will live to see the day when railways will replace all other methods of transportation in this country — when mail coaches will go by railway, and railroads will become the great highways for the king and his subjects. The time is coming when it will be cheaper for a workman to travel upon a railway than to walk on foot. I know there are great . . . difficulties to be faced; but what I have said will come to pass, as sure as you live. I only wish I may live to see the day, though I can scarcely hope for that, as I know how slow progress is, and with what difficulty I have been able to get the locomotive adopted, notwithstanding my ten years' successful experiment at Killingworth."

The first of the three engines to be delivered was engine

number one, *Locomotion*. These engines were built after Stephenson's latest plans, in his own factory at Newcastle. They did not differ much from the engines built eight or ten years before at Killingworth, but the workmanship was better.

A great crowd gathered to see the new railway opened. The locomotive was the center of attraction. Some came to rejoice, but many came to see the traveling engine blow up. A great procession was formed with engine number one at its head. Stephenson was the engineer. The train was made up of twelve cars loaded with coal and flour, a passenger coach for the directors and their friends, and twenty-one coal cars for other passengers, in all a train of thirty-four cars. At the head of the procession rode a man on a horse, carrying a banner with these words on it: "*Private Risk is the Public's Gain*." At the signal, off the great train started off. It moved at first at a rate of six to eight miles an hour. Stephenson finally decided to try the speed of the engine. He signaled the horseman to get out of the way, and put on the steam. The train now rushed toward Darlington at the rate of fifteen miles an hour, a marvelous speed for the day. The success of the engine excited great interest and admiration.

The number of passengers to be carried was a surprise. Not much had been thought of carrying passengers, and when the road was opened the company had only one passenger car, the *Experiment*. Other cars were soon added. The bodies of some old stagecoaches were bought and fastened to the wheels of coal cars. These passenger cars were first drawn by horses, but it was not long before one of Stephenson's locomotives could be seen steaming merrily along, drawing a train made up of several loaded coal cars and one or two of these humble passenger coaches.

Getting the Steam Railroad Accepted

The success of the Stockton and Darlington encouraged a group of men from England who contemplated building a railroad between Liverpool and Manchester. Some of them went to Killingworth to see Stephenson's engines. After seeing them, one of the men wrote: "Here is an engine that will before long effect a complete change in society. Mr. Stephenson is the greatest practical genius of the age. If he develops the full powers of that engine, his fame in the world will be equal to that of Watt." Naturally enough, when it was decided to build the new road, Stephenson was chosen engineer.

The new railroad stirred up much opposition, particularly among the owners of turnpikes and canals. The newspapers printed all sorts of ridiculous things. The

STEPHENSON SHOWING THE POSSIBILITIES OF THE LOCOMOTIVE

railroad would keep the cows from grazing and the hens from laying. The poisonous smoke from the locomotives would kill the birds, the grass, and the trees. The sparks would burn all the houses along the way. There would no longer be any use for horses — indeed, it would not be long before there would be no horses, and therefore oats and hay would be worthless. The price of land would be lowered, for it would be impossible to plow the neighboring fields, and dangerous to drive along the near-by wagon roads. Besides, any number of people would be killed by the bursting boilers. These fears seem ridiculous to us, but they were very real then.

There was also great opposition in Parliament when the bill to construct the road was secured. People were not ready to believe that an engine could race across the country, with hundreds of persons in its train, faster than the fleetest horse or dog could run. The very idea was absurd.

All sorts of amusing questions were asked: What would happen when the engine came to a curve in the track? How could an engine go in the face of a strong wind?

"Suppose now," said one member of Parliament, "that a cow got in the way of the engine; would not that be an awkward circumstance?"

"Yes," replied Stephenson, "very awkward for the cow."

Not only were Stephenson and his idea of a steam railroad ridiculed, but the best engineers of the day were called in to show that the road could not be built where Stephenson was going to build it. At one point the road passed over a great swamp, Chat Moss. "No engineer in his senses," said one of these experts, "would go through Chat Moss." Who but Mr. Stephenson would have thought of entering Chat Moss? It is ignorance. . . . Every part of the scheme shows that this man has applied himself to a subject of which he lacks knowledge."

Thus George Stephenson, "the engine wright of Killingworth," with only his practical knowledge to guide him and his genius to inspire him, battled for his ideas against the most learned men of the day. He stood alone. He was called "ignorant," "out of his senses," and "mad"; but as he said later, "I put up with every rebuff and went on with my plans, determined not to be put down."

THE ROCKET

When the Liverpool and Manchester railroad was nearly done, the directors were puzzled as to whether it was better to use stationary engines or locomotives. The engineers they consulted advised the use of a system of stationary engines placed at intervals along the way. Stephenson alone held out for the locomotive. With public opinion against him — for the most frightful stories were told about how dangerous and terrible the locomotive was — he urged his view upon the directors. Even in his darkest hour, he declared: "Locomotive railroads will, before many years, be the great highways of the world." At length the directors decided to offer a prize of two thousand dollars for the best locomotive. Four were entered for the prize: The *Novelty*, the

Sanspareil, the *Rocket*, and the *Perseverance*.

The *Rocket* was Stephenson's engine. It did not look much like the engines built at Killingworth or for the Stockton and Darlington, but the principles followed in making the *Rocket* were the same as in the earlier engines: few parts, and direct connection between the cylinders and the driving wheels. There was one important improvement. The earlier engines had a single large flue running through the boiler between the fire box and the smokestack. The *Rocket* was fitted with a boiler, in which there were twenty-five copper tubes, each three inches in diameter. This style of boiler made it easier to keep up the steam. The *Rocket* was therefore the best and fastest engine that Stephenson had built.

The trial was held at Rainhill, England, in 1829. Thousands of people, including many engineers and interested persons the world over, came to see the contest. The *Novelty* ran at the rate of twenty-four miles an hour, but it broke down. The *Sanspareil* traveled at an average speed of fourteen miles an hour, but its pumps got out of order and it had to stop. The *Perseverance* was unable to go more than four or five miles an hour, and was withdrawn from the contest. There yet remained the *Rocket*. On the *Rocket*, George Stephenson pinned all his hopes. He had battled for years for a great idea. He had done work and had faced difficulties that would have crushed many other men, but his courage had never failed him. Now, the *Rocket* would show the world whether or not he was "ignorant," "out of his senses," and "mad," and whether or not the steam railroad would become the "great highway of the world."

The *Rocket* made the trial trip at a maximum speed of twenty-nine miles an hour and at an average speed of fifteen. She met every condition of the contest. The spectators were greatly astonished at the wonderful performance.

The Liverpool and Manchester Railroad was opened to the public in 1830. It was justly looked upon as an event of national importance, and there was a big celebration. A great procession went from Liverpool to Manchester and back. Thousands upon thousands of people gathered along the way to view the great sight. Few of those who on that day saw a locomotive for the first time realized the importance of the invention made by the "engine wright of Killingworth."

In a very few years after that memorable contest at Rainhill, many counties saw the locomotives busy hauling raw materials to the mills and factories. Busy carrying the manufactured products where they were needed, and busy speeding passengers from place to place. The different sections of the same county were thus brought nearer together. Frontier regions were easily settled, new industries were developed, and new markets opened. The locomotive is therefore to be ranked as one of the world's great inventions, and George Stephenson as one of the world's great inventors.

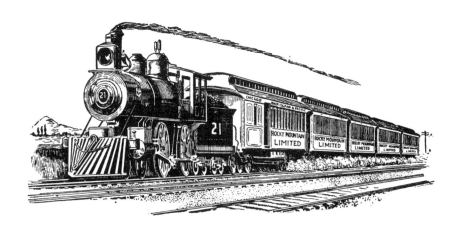

Comprehension Questions

1. How was Stephenson's father injured?
2. Where was George Stephenson born?
3. Why did the miners call Mr. Stephenson an "engine doctor?"
4. Did George Stephenson's poverty keep him from placing his child in a good school?
5. How did the locomotive change the way people lived?

First Steam Train (1831) on the Mohawk and Hudson Railroad, New York.

Chapter 4

Invention of the Electric Engine and Electric Locomotive

At the very time when Watt was working on his steam engine, Fulton on his steamboat, and Stephenson on his locomotive, men were beginning to learn about a new power that has since become more useful than steam. That power is electricity. Electric engines are now employed in mills and factories to drive all kinds of machinery, and electric locomotives are used on many railroads to pull long and heavy trains.

An electric engine includes two main parts: the dynamo, which produces or generates the electricity, and the motor, through which the electricity is converted into power. Before an electric engine could be constructed, it was necessary to discover a method of producing electricity in great quantities at small cost, or to invent the dynamo; and to find a way to change, with small loss, electricity into power, or to invent the motor. Besides, a great deal had to be learned about electricity itself. The electric engine, like most inventions, is therefore not the work of one man, but of many men working at different

83

times and in different countries.

MEN WHO FOUND ELECTRICITY

The Electric Battery

Almost everybody knows a little about electricity. Very often on a cold day, if one rubs his feet on a carpet and then touches another person, a crackling sound will be heard, and the person touched will receive a shock. Something like this happens when a cat's back is rubbed briskly. Despite these and other interesting things that have long been known, not much interest was taken in electricity so that it was not until the 19th century that much was really understood about it. Men did not begin to study electricity with care until about two hundred years before Washington became President.

Otto von Guericke, a German, was one of the first to study it carefully. He made the first machine to generate or produce electricity. His machine was merely a globe of sulphur supported so that he could turn it by a crank. When he placed his dry hand on the moving globe, it would attract bits of paper like a magnet. A similar machine was made later by placing a glass disk so that it could be easily turned, and by fixing many rubber or silk brushes so that they would rub against the revolving glass.

Alexander Volta, an Italian, was also a pioneer. He discovered in 1800 that two different metals in contact

FRICTIONAL ELECTRIC MACHINE: *A*, THE GLASS DISK; *P* AND *N*, THE PRIME AND NEGATIVE CONDUCTORS

with each other would produce an electric current. From this discovery, he invented an electric battery. It consisted of many cups piled on top of each other. In each cup he placed a disk of copper and a disk of zinc, covered with a brine of common table salt. The copper disk of the first cup was connected by a copper wire with the zinc disk of the second cup, and so on. A copper wire was also fastened to the copper disk of the first cup and one to the zinc disk of the last cup. On taking hold of these last two connecting wires a strong electric shock was felt, and the current continued to flow regularly. A battery like Volta's can be made without the cups by using a glass jar. It should be remembered, however, that the strength of the battery does not depend upon the size, but upon the number of the disks or plates.

Volta's battery was the first easy way found to produce electricity in quantities. Years of study and experiment have shown also that the metals used by Volta, copper and zinc, are the very best to employ in batteries. The so-called "dry battery," for example, used to work doorbells, was made until lately of copper and zinc disks covered with sand or sawdust, soaked in acid and sealed. The battery is today the most common of electrical appliances.

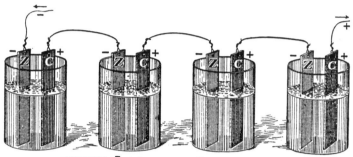

BATTERY: Z, ZINC PLATES; C, COPPER PLATES

Magnets are Useful

Most children at some time or other have owned a magnet, which as you know, will pick up or attract bits of paper, pins, or even metal filings. To make a compass, stroke a needle from end to end with one end of a magnet, and float the needle on a bit of cork. Iron filings arrange themselves in line like live soldiers, if a magnet is placed under a sheet of paper and the filings are spilled over the paper. It is

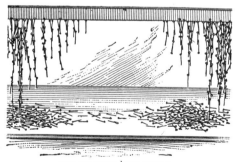

BAR MAGNET AND NAILS

the invisible currents of magnetism flowing around the magnet that make the filings squirm about.

For many hundreds of years, bar and horseshoe magnets were made by rubbing small iron bars over a natural magnet or loadstone. Loadstones are pieces of hard, black rock found in Asia Minor, China, and Japan. Naturally enough, magnets were looked upon as valuable possessions. Yet no practical use was made of them until about the middle of the twelfth century. A wise sailor placed a magnetized needle upon a float, to learn which way was north. Magnets are now used for many purposes. It was the study of them and their action that led to the invention of the dynamo, the telegraph, the telephone, and many other modern conveniences.

The Electromagnet

Sailors long ago noticed that when there was constant lightning, the needle of a compass danced about in all sorts of ways. The same dancing about of the needle was observed when a magnet was brought near a compass. These and other facts, like knives being made into magnets when a house was struck by lightning, aroused curiosity among scientists, to find out what connection there was between magnetism and electricity.

MARINER'S COMPASS

In the winter of 1820, it occurred to Professor Oersted of Copenhagen to try a new way to find the answer. On a table before him lay a compass and beside it was one of Volta's batteries. He connected the wires to complete the circuit of the battery, and brought one wire close to the side of the compass parallel to the needle. The needle swung around, just

ELECTROMAGNET

as if he had a magnet in his hand. When the current was sent through the wire toward the north, the needle moved to the left. When the current was sent through the wire toward the south, the needle swung to the right. Oersted saw he had made a discovery. Passing an electric current through a wire makes a magnet of the wire. "Magnetism," he said, "is but electricity in motion." Oersted's discovery was of importance, for it led to the invention of the electromagnet, one of the most useful of electrical inventions.

The first electromagnet was made by Sturgeon, an Englishman. He took a round bar of very soft iron and bent it in the shape of a horseshoe. Around this he wrapped a wire, and through the wire he passed an electric current. He varnished the core, as the iron bar is called, to keep the electricity from flowing off or away from it.

Sturgeon was surprised at the way the electromagnet worked. It was considerably stronger than a natural or permanent magnet of the same size. But the most surprising element was that the instant the current was turned on, the iron core became a magnet. When the current was turned off, the core practically ceased to be a magnet. It might be thought that this peculiar action of the electromagnet would make it a useless invention, but it is this very action that makes it so useful. If a needle or other object is picked up with a permanent magnet, the only way to get it off the magnet is to scrape or pull it off. To get it off an electromagnet, it is necessary only to break the electric current. The electromagnet is therefore under our control. To put it to work, we turn on the electric current; to make it stop working, we turn off the current. You do this every time you push the button of an electric doorbell or turn on and off a light in your home.

We can control also the power of the electromagnet, that is, the size of the load it will lift. The man who taught us how to do this was Joseph Henry, an American. Instead of varnishing the iron core as Sturgeon had done, to keep the electricity from flowing off, or to insulate it, Henry

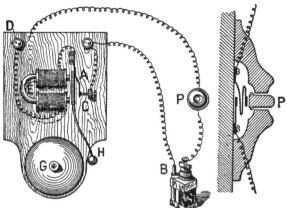

ELECTRIC DOORBELL: *G*, GONG; *E*, ELECTROMAGNET;
B, BATTERY; *P*, PUSH BUTTON

insulated the copper wire by covering it with a wrapping of silk. Instead of putting a single turn of wire round the iron core, he put many turns. On his first electromagnet he put thirty-five feet of wire, making about four hundred turns. These additional turns increased the strength of the magnet very much.

Henry found that the magnet was stronger when wound

91

with several separate coils of wire, the ends of each coil being connected with the battery. With a small battery, one of Henry's electromagnets lifted eighty-five pounds, and in 1831 he exhibited a magnet that lifted thirty-six hundred pounds. Thus by using a small or large battery, small or large iron cores, a few or many coils of wire, electromagnets of different strength can be made.

Henry was also the first to make the electromagnet do work at a distance, and to show us how it could be made useful. Mr. Henry explained his plan like this: "I arranged around one of the upper rooms in the Albany Academy a wire more than a mile in length, through which I was enabled to make signals by sounding a bell." This first electric bell was made up of a permanent magnet about ten inches long, supported on a pivot, and placed with one end between the two poles of an electric magnet. When the current was passed through the electromagnet, this caused the bar magnet to swing and strike the bell.

Small electromagnets by the millions are now in use. In connection with the electric battery, they ring our doorbells, sound alarms, move signals, and the like. Enormous lifting magnets are now employed to handle iron and steel. Some of these will lift as much as a hundred thousand pounds. Electromagnets are thus of themselves doing all kinds of work for us. In addition they are, as we shall see, an essential part of the telegraph, the telephone, and the dynamo.

The First Dynamo

The discovery that an electric current would produce a magnet prompted Michael Faraday, of the Royal Institution at London, to question, Will a magnet produce an electric current? He kept asking himself this question repeatedly. Oersted had changed electricity into magnetism. So Faraday tried doing the opposite, changing magnetism into electricity. He first tried to do this in 1822, but failed. He also failed in three other attempts. In the year 1831 he took up the problem for the fifth time. He coiled 220 feet of wire around a plasterboard tube and connected the ends of the coil to an instrument that would show if there was an electric current flowing. Taking a round bar magnet eight and a half inches long and three fourths of an inch in diameter, he thrust it quickly full length into the coil. The needle of the instrument showed that there was a current, but the current stopped when the magnet came to rest. He jerked the magnet out, and again the needle moved, but in the opposite direction. The needle swung back and forth each time the magnet was thrust in and out, but there was no movement when the magnet was still.

Faraday at last, after five attempts, succeeded in producing an electric current from a magnet. He saw why he had failed before. In his earlier attempts, the coil of wire and the magnet were left at rest. A magnet might lie in or by a coil of wire for a hundred years, and no electric current would come from it. The electric current, as Faraday had learned, is produced by the magnet when in motion, or when the wire coil breaks through the currents of magnetism coming from the magnet.

Faraday now saw how to make a new machine to generate electricity. A copper disk twelve inches in diameter and a fifth of an inch thick was fastened on a brass axle. This was so mounted that the disk could be turned rapidly. A powerful permanent horseshoe magnet was placed so the disk revolved between its two ends. A metal collector was held against the edge of the disk, and a second collector was fastened to the axle. Faraday turned the disk, and a steady current of electricity was produced. This was the first dynamo ever made.

By persevering until he found out how to produce an electric current from a magnet, Faraday blazed the way for some wonderful inventions. Without the dynamo to generate the electricity, we would not have electric lights, electric cars, electric railroads, or electric-driven machines in factories.

Michael Faraday was a poor boy who taught himself and became a great scientist. In this picture we see him at work in the laboratory of the Royal Institution, where he made many of his wonderful discoveries.

Making the Dynamo Useful

There are two parts to every dynamo, the magnet and the whirling disk. The electricity is produced by the disk, called the armature, breaking through or across the currents of magnetism coming from the magnet.

The currents of magnetism in Faraday's dynamo were supplied by a permanent magnet. But the electromagnet supplies a more powerful magnetic field than the strongest permanent magnet; therefore in all modern dynamos, electromagnets are employed. In the very largest dynamos there are several of these, each more powerful than the strongest one made by Henry.

The armature in Faraday's dynamo was merely a copper disk. Modern armatures are made up of a core or inner portion, and the windings of copper wire over the core. The core in the common armature is made up of a great number of very thin soft sheet-iron disks. Around these are wound many thousand turns of copper wire.

Between the time when Faraday made the first dynamo and the present, many men worked to make the dynamo useful, that is, to make one that would produce electricity in large quantities and at a small cost. Among these experimenters are to be counted Siemens of Germany, and Edison of America. Under the careful and patient work of these and other men, the simple dynamo of Faraday grew into the monsters of today. From these monster dynamos, hidden away in some remote power house, comes the electric current to light our homes and streets, to drive the machines of mills and factories, to haul passenger trains, and even to cook our food.

Modern power stations also use nuclear power to help drive the great dynamos that light up our homes and cities. You will learn more about atomic energy when you study science.

Finding the Motor

What was now needed was a machine, a motor, that would convert electricity into power that could be used to turn all kinds of machines. Toy motors were made as early as 1826. But a practical motor was not possible until the dynamo had been perfected, and cheap electricity was available.

In 1873 there was an Industrial Exhibition in Vienna, Austria, where a number of dynamos were displayed. One day an absent-minded workman connected the wires of a dynamo that was running to one that was standing still. To his surprise the armature began to spin around.

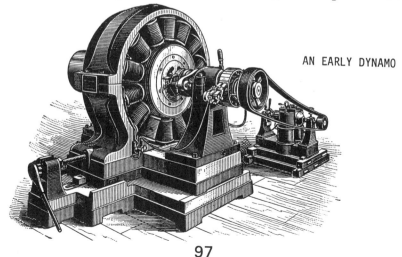

AN EARLY DYNAMO

97

AN ELECTRIC LOCOMOTIVE

It was thus discovered by accident that the dynamo, invented to produce electricity, could be used also to change electricity into power. The dynamo soon became a useful motor. Dynamos and motors are now built almost alike, but motors do not have to be as large and heavy as dynamos. So it is plain to see that the men who perfected the dynamo, without knowing it, also perfected the electric motor.

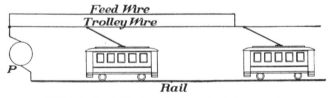

ELECTRIC TROLLEY CAR; *P* REPRESENTS THE POWER

The Dynamo and Motor at Work

The motor was immediately put to work. At the Industrial Exposition in Berlin in 1879, Dr. Siemens exhibited a small electric locomotive drawing a train of three small cars. The track, about a thousand feet long, was circular, and for this reason the first electric railway was called "Siemens' electrical merry-go-round." In 1881, Dr. Siemens built a street-car line a mile and a half long. A motor was fastened between the axles of an old horse car, and a dynamo exactly like the motor on the car was set up to furnish the electricity. The new electric line easily drove the trolley car through the streets. Electric street railways were soon being operated in all parts of the civilized world. Although electric trolley cars or trains are seldom seen today, they were an exciting improvement in transportation and served people well from 1885 to around 1960.

The American inventor Thomas Edison was quick to see the practical importance of the motor, and after hearing of Dr. Siemens' "electrical merry-go-round" began to work. His first electric locomotive was built early in 1880. It was made up of an ordinary flat dump car, on which was mounted a dynamo for a motor, known as "A Long-waisted Mary Ann." Improvements quickly followed, and it was not many months before his motors were ready to propel street cars. The first electric street railway in

America was built in Baltimore in 1885.

Edison was also among the first to see that electric locomotives could be built large enough to draw freight and passenger trains. By 1882 he had a big electric locomotive on exhibition at Menlo Park, New Jersey. Considerable use is now made of electric locomotives for hauling trains in and out of large cities; although most trains today run by gasoline or diesel engines. Steam locomotives are rarely seen today, except in museums, and have not been used regularly since the 1950s.

Besides being employed to propel trolley cars and locomotives, many motors are used in mills and factories to drive machinery. But it must not be supposed that all motors are large and powerful. They are of almost every imaginable size, from the great monsters in electric locomotives, down to the little motor that is just strong enough to run a sewing machine, or whirl an electric fan, or propel a toy engine.

Comprehension Questions

1. Who was Otto von Guericke and what did he study?
2. What practical use can magnets perform?
3. Who made the first electromagnet?
4. Who made the first dynamo?
5. What was Dr. Siemens' first electric railway called?

PART II

Inventions of Manufacture and Production

Chapter 5

The Invention of Spinning Machines: The Jenny, The Water Frame, and The Mule

While some men were working on inventions to furnish easy means of transportation, others were working on inventions to be used in the manufacture of articles of food, clothing, and shelter. The first of these inventions of manufacture and production were the spinning machines.

The Distaff and Spindle

The oldest spinning machine is the distaff and spindle. The spindle, the key part of all machine spinning, is a slender round piece of wood or iron about twelve inches long, tapering toward each end. On the upper end, there is a notch or slit in which to fasten the thread. The distaff is a round stick, three or four feet long. One end is used to hold the loose supply of wool or cotton. The other end of the stick is held under the left arm, and is often fastened in a girdle at the belt.

SPINNING WITH THE DISTAFF

When spinning with the distaff and spindle, the spinner pulls out a small piece of the loose wool or cotton and twists the end of it by hand. This finished end is fastened into the notch or slit of the spindle. The spinner sets the spindle whirling, by rolling it between her right hand and leg, or by a twisting motion of the hand. Then the spindle is left to whirl as it dangles at her side. With her left hand she holds the loose thread, and with her right hand she draws it out to the proper size, as it is twisted by the whirling spindle. When a thread two or three feet long is thus properly twisted, the thread is unfastened from the upper end of the spindle and wound on the lower end. This process is continued until all the material on the distaff is spun.

CARDING WOOL BY HAND

Until about the time of the Revolutionary War, all the woolen, flax, and cotton yarn used in the world was spun by this method. From such yarn were woven the clothes of peasant and prince alike. Even today, women may be seen in the Holy Land and in other remote parts of the world, spinning in this old-fashioned way.

The Spinning Wheel

The first improvement on this ancient method was the spinning wheel. This is a machine to whirl the spindle by turning a wheel. When the spinning wheel is employed, the cleaned wool or cotton is first carded, then twisted loosely, and finally spun into yarn. The carding is done with hand cards, big coarse nail brushes, about twelve inches long and five inches wide. The cotton is spread on one card and combed with another, until the fibers all lie in one direction. It is then taken off in fleecy rolls, about twelve inches long and three quarters of an inch thick. These short cardings are twisted on the spinning wheel into a loose thread, or roving, about the size of a candlewick. The rovings are wound on reels or bobbins, and finally spun into the finished yarn.

SPINNING WHEEL

The spinning wheel was a big advance over the distaff. The spindle could be kept whirling more rapidly and easily. The hands were free to fasten the short cardings together and draw them into rovings, or free to draw out the roving and to hold it while it was being twisted into yarn. One spinner could now spin as much yarn as a half dozen had done before. The yarn was more even, and better twisted.

Spinning wheels were to be found in most homes until about 1840, and even now many are to be seen in homes, preserved as curiosities. The mother always spun enough cotton and wool to supply the family with "linsey-woolsey" for clothes and yarns for socks.

James Hargreaves and the Spinning Jenny

The spinning wheel, which made only one thread at a time, was replaced by the spinning jenny, on which twenty, fifty, a hundred, and even a thousand threads can be spun at once. The inventor was James Hargreaves, an Englishmen.

Hargreaves sat pondering one day over a faster way to spin cotton. His wife was busy in another part of the small room. Her spinning wheel for some reason toppled over. The spindle, which was thrown from a horizontal to an upright position, continued to whirl. Hargreaves saw, by one of those flashes of thought that come to the genius, that, if many spindles were placed upright side by side, and a way found to draw out the rovings as they were twisted, many threads could be spun by one pair of

105

hands at once. The idea of the spinning jenny was thus born. The invention was named jenny after Hargreaves' wife.

One person can spin with a jenny as much yarn as a dozen people can spin using the old spinning wheel. The yarn, too, is of better quality.

The first jenny was completed about 1767. Hargreaves tried to keep his invention a secret, and to use it only in his home. But he was tempted to make a few jennies to sell, to buy necessities for his children. In time, the spinners learned that he had a wonderful spinning machine with which one person could do as much work as a dozen people with spinning wheels. People at that time were not used to machines. It was the age of handwork; they had not yet learned that machines in the end create more employment and better wages. They only saw that this invention would lessen the number of spinners needed, and would deprive them of work. So the spinners, who as a rule were women, with their husbands and friends, rose up against the inventor. A mob broke into his house and broke all the jennies that could be found, and Mr. Hargreaves had to flee for his life.

To protect his invention, he took out a patent in 1770, but this did no good. The spinning jenny was so easy to

HARGREAVES' SPINNING JENNY

make that the manufacturers, quick to see its merits, made their own, and refused to pay any royalty on them. Thus it came about that Hargreaves received nothing for an invention that for forty years was the principal machine used in spinning cotton yarn. He did not, however, live and die in poverty, as the story is often told. From a yarn factory of which he was part owner, he made a good living for himself and his family.

Richard Arkwright and the Water Frame

Cloth is usually made from two kinds of thread, the warp running lengthwise, and the woof running crosswise. Warp is a stronger thread than woof. Neither the spinning wheel nor the jenny made a cotton thread strong enough for warp. The warp in all cotton cloth up to this time was for this reason linen, and only the woof cotton. Linen thread costs more than cotton thread, and this made cotton cloth more expensive than if both the warp and woof were cotton. If cotton cloth was to be cheaper, a way had to be found to spin a cotton thread strong enough for warp. The man who succeeded was Richard Arkwright, also an Englishman.

Richard Arkwright was the youngest of thirteen children in a poor family. If he ever took the time to learn, it was only for a short time. To make up for his lack of early education, Arkwright, when more than fifty years old and when working from five o'clock in the morning until nine at night, took an hour each day to study English grammar, and another hour to improve his spelling and writing.

When a boy, he did all sorts of odd jobs, and finally became a barber. Even as a barber, he showed that he was a man of enterprise. The usual price for a shave was two cents. Arkwright made his price a penny. When the other barbers lowered their price to one penny, he advertised "a good shave for a half penny."

By the time he was thirty, Arkwright had enough of shaving. He began buying and selling hair to be used in wigs, which were stylish at the time. He went about the

ARKWRIGHT SELLING HAIR TO A WIGMAKER

country from cottage to cottage, and became an expert in getting young girls to part with their long, glossy locks. He also came into possession of a secret way of dyeing hair, which added to its value. As a dealer in hair, he gained a sort of reputation, for the wigmakers pronounced "Arkwright's hair the best in the country."

As a barber and as a dealer in hair, Arkwright had a good opportunity to talk with people about spinning, about the lack of yarn, and about the different spinning machines that were being invented. Whether he got the idea from one of his customers, or from other inventions, or whether he was wise enough to see the need himself, he made up his mind to invent a spinning machine. Like other inventors before and after him, he began to neglect his regular business. Instead of saving money, he spent more than he earned. So before the first successful model was completed, he had spent all his savings, and his family was poor.

Arkwright's machine, patented in 1769, spun cotton, flax,

ARKWRIGHT'S FIRST SPINNING FRAME

or wool. Pairs of rollers drew out the rovings, and flying spindles did the rest. The machine is called the water frame because it was first driven by water power, but a better name is the roll-drawing spinning machine.

His invention was even a greater one than Hargreaves'.

The water frame spun such a strong thread that it could be used for warp. Cloth could now be made for the first time entirely of cotton, and it was not long before English calicoes made their appearance. The thread was also so strong that it could be used for knitting cotton socks. Hargreaves' spinning jenny was suited only to spin thread from rovings, while the rovings had to be twisted on the spinning wheel. But the water frame twisted the rovings as well as spun the finished yarn. The water frame therefore did away with the spinning wheel in factories, but not with the spinning jenny. The spinning jenny continued to be used to make the softer threads for woof, while the water frame was employed to twist rovings and to spin the harder and stronger yarns.

Like Hargreaves, Arkwright received next to nothing for his invention, which eventually gave the world a machine that spun the warp for the cloth used by millions of people.

But he did not stop with the water frame. He went on and on, making one invention after another, until he had many machines, best described by calling them a cotton-yarn factory. The uncleaned cotton was put into the first of these, and it came out of the last, the water frame, as snow-white, well-twisted thread.

Arkwright was not only a great inventor, but he proved to be a good business man. For a time, he made little from his inventions or from a cotton manufactory of which he

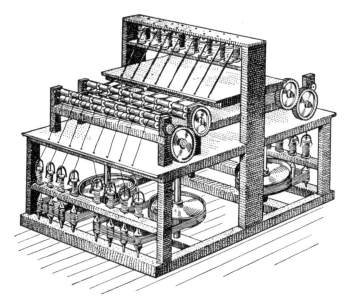

ARKWRIGHT WATER FRAME

HAND LOOM

was part owner. It was not long, however, before wealth began to flow his way. He finally became one of the most important cotton-mill owners in England, and for several years controlled the market price of cotton yarn. Shortly before his death he was made a knight.

Samuel Crompton and the Mule

The spinning jenny spun good woof. The water frame spun good warp. But neither of these inventions spun yarn fine enough to weave muslin. All the muslin of the day came from India. The weavers from India were so skillful that they could make the very finest yarn, even on

113

the spinning wheel. The spinning machine that broke India's hold on the muslin trade was the mule, invented in 1779 by Samuel Crompton, another Englishman.

From early childhood Samuel helped his widowed mother, who supported her only son and her two daughters by keeping a cow or two, by growing a good garden, and by spinning and weaving. Samuel's "little legs became accustomed to the loom almost as soon as they were long enough to touch the treadles." Yet he went to school regularly, and was given a good education. Going to school did not, however, relieve him from a certain amount of spinning and weaving each day. His mother was in her way loving and kind, but woe unto Samuel if his daily amount of spinning and weaving was not done. Samuel learned the importance of hard work.

Whether or not the eight-spindle jenny used by Samuel was a poor one, much of his time was taken up in "mending the ever-breaking ends of his miserable yarn." To escape the reproach of his exacting mother, it kept him forever busy to do the allotted amount of spinning and weaving. Then, too, Samuel was an excellent workman. He longed to weave cloth as beautiful and delicate as the muslins of India. When he was twenty-one years of age, he began to think about how a better spinning machine than the jenny could be made.

The Invention of Spinning Machines

Most inventors are inspired by the hope that from their inventions they will gain both fame and wealth. From childhood, Crompton had been very sheltered. Spinning and weaving was not then, as now, done in big factories. He knew very little about the world, and less about how valuable a great invention might be.

Crompton worked on the new machine from the time he was twenty-one until he was twenty-six. He says: "The next five years had . . . added to my labor as a weaver . . . , a continuous endeavor to make a more perfect spinning machine. Though often baffled, I as often renewed the attempt, and at length succeeded to my utmost desire, at the expense of every shilling I had in the world." It might be added, at the expense also of the goodwill of his neighbors.

Strange sounds were heard coming from Crompton's home. Lights were seen at all hours of the night. The rumor went about that the house was haunted. It was soon discovered that Crompton was the ghost. But when relieved of their fears of a ghost, the neighbors found that they had in their midst a "conjuror," the term of contempt applied to an inventor. So Crompton became an object of suspicion.

Hardly was the first mule completed, when the anti-machine riots of 1779 broke out. Mobs of spinners and weavers went about crying, "Men, not machines." Rioters went everywhere, destroying all the jennies and water frames they could lay their hands on, especially all jennies having more than twenty spindles. The usual number was eighty. Crompton knew that his invention would arouse the rioters even more than the jenny or the water frame. Fearing that they would destroy it, he took it to pieces and hid it in the attic of his workroom. There it lay for weeks, before he had courage to bring it down and put it together. He now learned for the first time what his machine would do. After a little practice, he could spin yarn on it fine enough for the most delicate muslin.

His invention is called the mule, because it combines in one machine the best points in Arkwright's water frame and the best points in Hargreaves' spinning jenny. Before this, the greatest length of yarn ever spun from a pound of cotton was less than 70,000 yards. With the mule, it was possible to spin, from a single pound of cotton, a thread 300,000 yards in length.

Crompton's only idea in inventing the mule, as stated before, was to make a machine for his own use. The way before him now seemed clear, and he married. For a few months he prospered, and he and his wife were happy.

But such a valuable invention could not be kept a secret long. Crompton's yarn was the finest that came to the market, and he received the highest price for it.

His neighbors began to ask, "How can Sam Crompton make such fine yarn? He must have a new kind of spinning machine." Some of them went to his home to see. Crompton, of course, tried to keep them from learning about his invention. He wanted to be left alone, so that he might reap the fruits of his labor. He even went as far as to put a special lock on his workroom, and to put screens at the windows. But his neighbors were not to be outdone. They called at unexpected times. They even brought ladders and looked over the screens. One fellow, it is said, lay in the loft overhead for days, and peeped down through a knot hole.

This spying almost drove Crompton mad. He even thought of breaking his invention to pieces. "A few months reduced me," he afterward wrote, "to the cruel necessity either of destroying my machine altogether or of giving it up to the public. It was not in my power to keep it and work it. To destroy it, I could not think of that; to give up that for which I had labored so long was cruel. I had no patent nor the means of purchasing one. In preference to destroying it, I gave it to the public."

To induce him to do this, some manufacturers promised to raise a liberal purse. The total subscription amounted to only about three hundred and thirty dollars, but no sooner was the invention made public than the subscriptions stopped. Worse still, some subscribers refused to pay what they had promised. Crompton scarcely received enough to build a new mule, for he had loaned the manufacturers the one he was working with, to use as a model in making others.

The first mule was a crude machine, and had less than twenty or thirty spindles. Several years of improvements turned it into a beautifully constructed machine that could carry a thousand spindles. The mule, like the jenny, was first worked by a spinner, but eventually it was converted to work automatically. The improved mule became the most wonderful of all spinning machines. It was used the world over to spin both the warp and the woof of all the finer kinds of cotton goods.

Crompton did not go wholly unrewarded, however. In part payment for the benefits of his invention, Parliament voted him twenty-five thousand dollars. But this was soon wasted by his sons in business. He became very poor a few years before his death. Some admiring friends then raised by private subscription a fund that gave him an annual income of three hundred dollars. Without this, he would probably have died in poverty since his lazy and foolish sons refused to perform their God-given duty to care for their father in his old age.

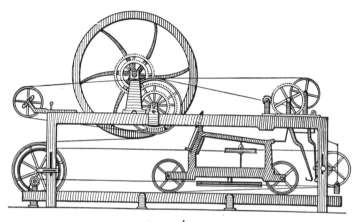

CROMPTON'S MULE

Comprehension Questions

1. What was the name of the machine that replaced the spinning wheel?
2. Who invented the machine known as the mule?
3. What type of problems did the inventor of the mule encounter?
4. Prior to the invention of the mule, where was muslin normally made?
5. Did the inventor of the mule become rich?

Chapter 6

Eli Whitney and the Invention of the Cotton Gin

With the inventions of Hargreaves, Arkwright, and Crompton, huge amounts of cheap cotton yarn could be spun. Then the power loom was invented, which lowered the cost of weaving. The age of cheap clothing seemed at hand, when the poor as well as the rich could afford enough clothes to be well dressed, clean, and warm. One difficulty stood in the way, however: the lack of cheap cotton.

The primary sources of cotton at that time were Asia and the West Indies. Very little cotton was raised in the United States, because of the great cost of separating the seeds from the fiber or lint. It took ten to fifteen days to harvest five to eight hundred pounds of green seed cotton from one acre of land. Then came the long tedious job of removing the seeds. It takes four pounds of green seed cotton to produce a single pound for the market. The seeds were picked out by hand. This was usually done in the evening, after the regular work of the day. Then the slaves — father, mother, and children — would sit in a circle around a torch and pick seeds from cotton.

PICKING COTTON SEED BY HAND

An American, Eli Whitney, invented a machine to do this work. Because of his invention, the United States is now one of the greatest cotton-producing countries in the world.

Whitney's cotton gin easily ranks in importance with the jenny of Hargreaves, the water frame of Arkwright, and the mule of Crompton. These four inventions were the foundation of the cotton industry for many years. Even modern spinning and weaving machines are patterned somewhat after these inventions. To spin and weave cotton, hamlets have grown into cities, such as Manchester in England, and Lowell in Massachusetts. Great territories, such as our Southern States, have been given over to the cultivation of cotton. Special trucks and railroad lines have been built to carry cotton from the fields to the mills. Millions of people earn their daily bread from raising or weaving cotton, or from selling the finished goods. To have had a part in the growth of a great industry is no slight honor.

BIRTHPLACE OF ELI WHITNEY

Boyish Traits of Whitney

Eli Whitney was born at Westboro, Massachusetts, in 1765. His parents lived on a farm, and belonged to that sturdy class who provide well for their children, and train them to be industrious, saving, honest, and honorable.

123

These virtues boys and girls must have if they are to lead clean lives, be useful, and be truly successful.

WHITNEY AND THE WATCH

As a mere boy, Eli had a passion for pulling things apart, to see how they were made and how they worked. His sister tells this story: "His father's watch was the greatest piece of mechanism Eli had yet seen. He was very anxious to look inside it and to examine the works, but was not permitted to do so. One Sunday morning, observing that his father was going to a Church meeting, and was leaving at home the wonderful little machine, he . . . made believe that he was sick, as an apology for not going to church. When the family was out of sight, he flew to the room where the watch hung, and taking it down, he was so delighted with . . . the movements of the wheels, that he took it to pieces before he thought about what he was doing. His father was a stern parent, and he . . . would have been punished . . . for his idle curiosity and lying, had the mischief been found out. However, Eli put the

124

watch back together so neatly that his father never discovered . . . what he had done, until Eli told him and asked forgiveness many years afterward."

Eli was equally fond of making things. "Our father," writes the sister, "had a workshop . . . and a variety of tools, also a lathe, this gave my brother an opportunity . . . to learn the use of tools when very young . . . He was always making something in the shop, and seemed not to like working on the farm. On one occasion, after the death of our mother, when our father had been absent from home two or three days, on his return he asked of the housekeeper what the boys had been doing. She told him what B. and J. had been doing. 'But what has Eli been doing?' said he. She replied, 'He has been making fiddles.' 'Ah! I fear Eli will have to take his portion in fiddles!'"

Eli was not more than fifteen or sixteen years of age when he began to put his gift for making things to practical use. It was the time of the Revolutionary War. Nails, made then by hand, were scarce and brought a good price. Eli proposed to his father that he give him the needed tools to make nails. This the father did, and it was not long before Eli was supplying all the neighbors for miles around. Besides, he put new blades in broken knives, and did different kinds of curious jobs in a way that exceeded the skill of the country smiths. When the war ended, it was no longer profitable to make nails, but fashion came to young Whitney's rescue. The ladies of the time used long pins to fasten on their bonnets. Whitney made these pins with such skill and finish that he had a monopoly of the trade. He also built up a good business making walking canes.

When almost nineteen, Whitney began to wish for a better education than could be obtained in the district school. By working in his shop, and by teaching school for two winters, he saved enough money to enter college. He entered Yale University in the fall of 1789. When a boy like Whitney enters college now, he is almost certain to take a course in mechanical engineering. But when Whitney went to Yale, there was no such course. There was only one course, the classical, made up for the most part of Greek, Latin, and mathematics, with a little science. Though Whitney lacked opportunity at Yale to prepare himself to become an engineer, he never lost his interest in making things.

One day a teacher found a piece of apparatus out of order, and said in Whitney's presence, "I am sorry, but it must go abroad for repair, to the shop it came from."

Whitney replied, "I think I might mend it."

Within a week the machine was as good as new.

A Visit to the South

About the only opening for a college graduate in 1792, when Whitney finished his studies at Yale, was to become a minister, a lawyer, or a teacher. Few college graduates thought then of going into business, and there was little or no engineering work. Whitney decided, at least for a time, to take up teaching, so he secured a place to tutor the children of a wealthy gentleman at Savannah, Georgia. On the same boat for Savannah, was Mrs. Nathanael Greene,

WHITNEY REPAIRING THE CHILDREN'S TOYS

127

widow of the famous General Greene. Mrs. Greene saw that Whitney was a young man of character, and the two became well acquainted before they reached Georgia.

When Whitney arrived at Savannah, he found that his employer, instead of being willing to pay one hundred dollars a year and board for the teaching of his children, as he had promised to do, was now unwilling to pay more than fifty dollars a year. Whitney refused to take the position. This left him in a strange city, without friends and almost without money. Mrs. Greene, on hearing of his troubles, invited him to her plantation, some twelve miles from Savannah.

Whitney was not long in winning the hearts of Mrs. Greene's children. His skillful fingers made for them many wonderful toys, and he repaired others that were broken. Nor did Mrs. Green's respect for Whitney grow less as she came to know him better. She soon learned also that she was entertaining an inventor of the first rank. One evening, while making a piece of embroidery on a frame called a tambour, she complained that the frame tore the delicate silk threads of her work. An evening or two later, Whitney presented her with a frame to do the same work, but made in a different way. The new frame was much better than the old one, and Mrs. Greene wanted to know where he had obtained it. To her surprise, he replied, "Oh! I just got it out of my head."

Early in January 1793, three former comrades of General Greene's visited Mrs. Greene. Being planters, they talked of farming and about what could and what could not be raised at a profit. They all agreed that much of their upland would raise good cotton, but that there was no profit in growing cotton, because it cost so much to separate the seeds from the lint. They desperately needed a machine to do away with this tedious and costly work. Mrs. Greene then said, "Gentlemen, why don't you ask my young friend, Mr. Whitney; he can make anything."

Whitney was called in, but when he learned what the planters wanted, he assured them that he did not know how to make such a machine. Still, to have the need pointed out to him, and to be asked to make a machine, aroused all the inventive genius there was in him.

Inventing the Cotton Gin

The very next day saw him on his way to Savannah to get some cotton with seeds. Returning, he told Mr. Miller, who was then manager of Mrs. Greene's plantation, and afterward her husband, what he intended to do. Mrs. Greene also became aware of the secret. They were scarcely less enthusiastic than Whitney himself. A room in the basement of the house served for a shop. Here they set up a workbench and assembled a few common tools. This done, Whitney began to work.

In Asia, the West Indies, and along the coast in the South, a crude kind of roller gin was in use, made of two rollers, which revolved very close together. The seed cotton put in on one side was drawn between the revolving rollers, as clothes used to be drawn through a clothes wringer. The seeds too large to go between the rollers were broken off, and dropped down on the opposite side from the cotton. This roller gin performed fairly well for the black seed cotton of Asia and the West Indies, and what little was raised along the coast in the South, as it has a long fiber, and large seeds loosely attached. With a roller gin one man could clean from fifty to sixty pounds of black seed cotton in a day.

But the roller gin would not clean the green seed cotton raised on the uplands of Georgia, which has a short fiber and small seeds firmly attached. Whitney, however, obtained a valuable suggestion from the roller gin. He thought it would be a good idea to make a machine that would shove or thrust the cotton through slits so narrow that when the cotton was pushed through, the seeds would be torn off, just as they were broken off when the cotton was drawn between the rollers of the roller gin. How could such a machine be made?

Whitney's first successful gin had a hopper to hold the cotton. Iron bars placed close together in pairs formed one side of the hopper, and heavy boards the other. Reaching well up into the hopper was a wooden cylinder, armed with rows of wire teeth curved slightly back from the direction in which the cylinder moved. When the cylinder turned, the short wire teeth grabbed small bunches of cotton, and thrust these through the slits between the iron bars. The pressure of the cotton on the sides of the slits pulled off the seeds, which dropped into a trough. The cotton fiber was drawn on through the slits. Most of the fiber fell from the wire teeth. What still held on was pushed off by big brushes on the left of the machine, which revolved in an opposite direction and four times as fast as the cylinder.

Whitney did not make a machine like this at first. The hopper of iron gratings and boards was clear in his mind from the start. The part which gave him the most trouble was the teeth of the cylinder. His first idea was to use teeth like those of a circular saw. But he did not have any thin iron plates available that were strong enough to make such teeth. Fortunately, there arrived at this time a coil of heavy iron wire, purchased to make a bird cage for Mrs. Greene's daughter. The sight of this wire suggested to

Whitney making wire teeth. The wire was too large and had to be drawn smaller. This was slow work with Whitney's crude tools. But he was an expert. Had he not drawn thousands of bonnet pins? Trial after trial was made with wire teeth of different lengths and shapes. He finally learned that teeth about an inch long, and curved slightly back from the direction in which the cylinder turned, were the best at taking out all the seeds without greatly injuring the fiber. But every now and then the teeth would become clogged, and it was hard work to get the cotton off. Mrs. Greene one day saw Whitney working away, cleaning the clogged teeth.

"Why don't you clean the cotton off this way?" And she began to brush away with a hearth brush.

"Just the thing!" exclaimed Whitney. A short time later, a revolving brush was set up just behind the toothed cylinder and this improved the invention.

Toward the end of the winter of 1793, Whitney completed his first machine. It was hardly finished before Mrs. Greene invited several friends in to see it work. With Whitney's little gin, scarcely harder to turn by hand than a grindstone, one man could clean as much cotton as fifty men cleaned in the old way.

The planters looked on in amazement. They were quick to see that, with this machine to take out the seeds, they could raise cotton at a good profit. They congratulated Whitney on his ingenuity. They urged him to get a patent at once, telling him that his invention was sure to bring him wealth and honor. Whitney was too much of a Yankee to be averse either to wealth or to honor. He and Mr. Miller entered into a partnership to take out a patent, and to make and sell gins. Mr. Miller was to supply the money.

So enthusiastic were the planters over the outlook for raising cotton that it was hard for them to keep such a secret to themselves. Before long the news was all over

Georgia. Crowds gathered from all parts of the state. The machine had not yet been patented, and Mr. Miller would not let them see it. One night, the shed in which it was kept was broken open and the machine carried away. It thus came about that gins were made after Whitney's idea before he secured his patent.

Seeking the Reward

Miller and Whitney, as the firm was called, made a mistake often made by young men. They wanted to make much money, and they wanted to make it quickly. Instead of asking a modest sum for the use of a gin and letting anyone make one who wanted to, they proposed to build and own all the gins that were to be used. For ginning the cotton, they proposed to take from the planters each third pound of clean cotton. This was an exorbitant charge. The very best cotton planters resented such a price and were angry at what they called a monopoly.

The gins built for use at this time had as a rule eighty rows of teeth, and were worked by two horses or oxen, or by water power. With such a gin, one man could clean five thousand pounds of seed cotton, or prepare from a thousand to twelve hundred pounds of clean cotton for the market in a day. That is as much as a thousand men could clean by hand. Is it any wonder that these two young men had visions of great and immediate wealth?

From the first, Miller and Whitney found it difficult to obtain the money they needed to build a factory and to procure tools and materials. To build gins in large numbers also proved a bigger undertaking than either of the partners had supposed. In those days when the cotton gin was young, there were few skilled mechanics, and there were no automatic lathes, or planes, or drills. Everything was done by hand.

Then, too, the young men had many problems. The factory that they built at New Haven, Connecticut, was hardly in good working order before it caught fire, and building, machinery, and finished gins were destroyed. Though steps were taken at once to build a new factory, this accident lessened the number of gins they were able to make. As late as 1796, they had only thirty gins of their own at work in the whole state of Georgia.

Meanwhile, the production of cotton in the South increased quickly. In 1792, the year before the invention of the cotton gin, 138,000 pounds of cotton were raised and sent out of the United States. In 1793, about 487,000 pounds were exported; in 1794, about 1,000,000 pounds; and in 1800, about 17,000,000 pounds.

The planters put in cotton, expecting to take the seeds out of it with one of Whitney's gins. Even if the planters had been willing to pay one pound out of each three for ginning — and there were many who were not - Miller and Whitney did not have and could not possibly have built gins enough to clean the entire cotton crop. What were the planters to do? Were they to let their cotton stand in the field and spoil, because there was no gin owned and made by Miller and Whitney at hand to clean it? Were they to stop raising cotton, because two young men had a patent on a great invention, and had a foolish idea about how to make a fortune out of it? The planters did what it was natural to expect them to do. They had some nearby carpenter and blacksmith make them a gin, and with it they cleaned their cotton.

Seeing what the planters were doing, Miller and Whitney gave up the idea of making and owning all the gins used. They now tried to collect a royalty of two hundred dollars a year on each gin in operation. A tax of two hundred dollars a year on a machine that a local carpenter and blacksmith can make at a cost of from fifty to one hundred dollars, and which had cost the inventor but three months of effort, was excessive. A few planters paid the fee, but most of them refused. An agent sent out through Georgia to collect these royalties was not able to get money even enough to pay his own expenses.

Miller and Whitney had other troubles quite as serious as trying to collect royalties from planters. Hodgen Homes, of Georgia, patented a gin, called the "saw gin." It was made like Whitney's, except that dull teeth like those of a circular saw were used instead of wire teeth. Homes's "saw gin" took out the seeds better than Whitney's, and did less injury to the cotton. Naturally, people preferred it to Whitney's, and it was on the point of driving his machine from the field.

Whitney's first idea, you will remember, was to use saw teeth. But iron plates thin and strong enough to make saw teeth were not to be had, so he fell back on wire teeth. Whitney therefore felt that Homes was using his idea, and he brought suit in court to prevent the making of "saw gins." Unfortunately for Whitney, in his application for a patent nothing was said either in words or in drawings about saw teeth. For this reason, it was hard for Whitney to prove that the idea of using saw teeth belonged to him and not to Homes. He finally succeeded and Homes's patent was taken away.

Finding it difficult to keep others from making and selling gins after their model, and being unable to collect a royalty from the planters, Miller and Whitney now thought it would be best to sell the right to use their gin to the states themselves. In this way they received altogether ninety thousand dollars. Much of this sum was spent for lawyers' fees and other expenses. What little remained made up in large part Whitney's reward for his invention, and for years of worry and disappointment.

If the cotton gin failed to bring to Whitney the wealth of which he dreamed, it did bring great wealth to the South. The invention came at a time when the old products of the South, such as tobacco and rice, were cheap, and when it was hard to find profitable use for her lands. The cotton gin created for her a new crop, "King Cotton," in which there were enormous profits. These profits made the South rich, adding millions of dollars to the value of her plantations.

Making Rifles

However, Whitney was destined to become rich. He was too gifted a man to be crushed by disappointment over his first invention. As soon as he saw that there was little chance of getting paid for the cotton gin, he looked for a new project where he could use his genius for mechanics and invention, and where by industry and economy he might perhaps make the fortune that he once thought was all but in his hands. He began to make rifles for the government, and in 1798 he built a factory at New Haven, Connecticut.

Whitney's genius for invention showed itself no less in manufacturing rifles than in making the first cotton gin. Before his day, one man made the metal receiver of a gun, another carved the stock, another drilled out the barrel,

FLINTLOCK GUN

and so on. Each workman had considerable skill, did everything by hand, and made one entire piece. But no two receivers, or stocks, or barrels were exactly alike. If the receiver of a rifle broke, no other receiver would fit; a new part had to be made for that particular gun.

Whitney changed all this. He invented power machines to cut, to file, to drill, and to bore, which did away with hand machines. He divided the making of a rifle into about a hundred different parts, and divided the making of each part into many single steps, so that little skill was needed by a workman to do any one of them. Each part was made after a pattern, so that all receivers, all stocks, and all barrels were exactly alike. If part of a rifle broke, it could be replaced at slight cost, with a new piece from the factory, which was sure to fit.

Whitney was the first to manufacture anything in this new way. His ideas were followed by others, and similar methods are now used in making all kinds of things. So, Whitney is often called the "father of modern factory methods." He will always be honored, of course, as the inventor of the cotton gin, but his right to fame rests no less on what he taught the world about the use of machines in the making of common things.

Comprehension Questions

1. How did the cotton gin help to enhance the United States cotton industry?
2. Where was Eli Whitney born?
3. How did Eli Whitney earn a living during the Revolutionary War?
4. What was the "saw gin?"
5. How did Whitney improve the manufacture of rifles?

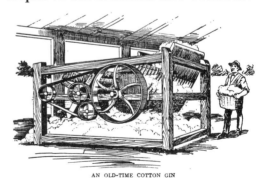

AN OLD-TIME COTTON GIN

Chapter 7

Elias Howe and the
Invention of the Sewing Machine

Sewing is older than spinning or weaving. Centuries ago people learned how to sew together pieces of fur. They used a pointed bone or a thorn to make a hole; through this they pushed a coarse thread or leather thong, making a knot at each hole.

It took thousands of years for sewing to get beyond the shoemaker's way of doing it. Women learned, to be sure, how to make different stitches, such as the plain seam and the hem. Fine spun thread took the place of coarse twist and the leather thong. The bone needle with an eye at one end and a point at the other gave way to delicate steel needles. Still, sewing continued to be done by hand, stitch after stitch, first one, then another, hour after hour. Even up to the days of our own great-grandmothers, the family sewing continued to be the burden of the home.

Men in England, France, and America worked for years to relieve the home of this drudgery. Machine after machine was invented, but each of these was a failure. Not until

1846 did an inventor succeed in doing for the sewing machine what Watt did for the steam engine, Stephenson for the locomotive, and Fulton for the steamboat. The inventor was Elias Howe, who was born at Spencer, Massachusetts, in 1819.

His Early Training

Howe's father was a farmer, who, in addition to his farm, had a gristmill, sawmill, and a shingle machine. To the farm at Spencer, the neighbors brought their wheat and corn to be ground into flour and meal, and their logs to be sawed into lumber or split into shingles. Yet with all his labor, the income of the father was small, and supplied only a modest living to a family of eight children.

HOWE HELPING AT THE MILL

In the pleasant surroundings of this New England farm, Elias Howe spent his childhood. Many were the rambles through the near by woods for squirrels and nuts. The brook running through the farm afforded good swimming and fishing in the summer, and good skating in the winter. When he was old enough, the boy did all sorts of simple farm work, and helped at odd jobs about the mills and shingle machine. Each winter found him busy at school. Elias thus grew up, a happy, good-natured, play-loving boy. If his chances to obtain an education at the district school were not very good, this lack was made up, at least in part, by the opportunities he had to see and know trees, plants, and animals; and by being able to learn how to do things with his hands, and to become acquainted with tools.

Becomes a Mechanic

The father's first thought was to make Elias a farmer. At eleven years of age the boy was apprenticed, as was the custom of the day, to a neighbor, where he was to live and work until he was twenty-one. Elias was not strong, having a lame foot. This made farm work hard for him. After trying it for a year, he decided to give it up. Returning home he went to work in his father's mills, where he remained until he was sixteen.

About this time a friend of Elias's came back to Spencer from Lowell, Massachusetts. He told what a big and busy place Lowell was, and how Elias could get employment there and earn more money, and earn it more easily than at Spencer. Elias's ambition was thus stirred to go to Lowell and become a mechanic. It was not his liking for machinery that led him to go; it was the thought that a mechanic makes his living at easy work. Elias was not a lazy boy, but hard work so taxed his strength as to be very distressing to him. It was, therefore, natural for him to want to avoid hard physical labor. His physical weakness led him also to do considerable thinking about how to do things with the least possible labor.

At Lowell, Elias was taken on as a learner in a factory for making cotton machinery. Here he worked for two years, until the factory shut down. Drifting to Cambridge he found, after a few months, a place much to his liking with Ari Davis. Davis kept a shop for making and repairing watches, clocks, surveying instruments, and the like. Besides, his head was full of ideas of great machines. To hear him talk, it seemed not at all difficult to make a profitable invention. Naturally almost every workman in his shop had the inventor's bee. Still, Ari Davis's shop was not a bad place for a young country boy to be. It was there that Elias Howe gained the suggestion that led to the invention of the first successful sewing machine.

One day in the year 1839, a man came to the shop who

was working to perfect a knitting machine. He was at his wit's end, and brought the model to Davis to see if he could help him.

Davis in his extravagant way said, "What are you bothering yourself with a knitting machine for? Why don't you make a sewing machine?"

"I wish I could," replied the caller, "but it can't be done."

"Oh, yes, it can," said Davis. "I can make a sewing machine myself."

"Well, said the other, "you do it, and you will have a fortune."

These remarks were taken by most of the work-men as idle boasts. Not so with Howe. He kept thinking about the idea of "inventing a sew-ing machine and making a fortune."

As the boy pondered, this resolution slowly took form in his mind: "I will invent that sewing machine and win that fortune."

The First Sewing Machines

To Howe, a country boy just turning twenty, the idea of a sewing machine was new, but the idea was not new to the world. As early as 1790, Thomas Saint, an Englishman, took out a patent on a machine for "quilting, stitching, and sewing, and for making shoes, and other articles . . . ."

Saint's machine had some of the features of good sewing machines today. Notice the overhanging arm and the block-like plate on which to place the material to be

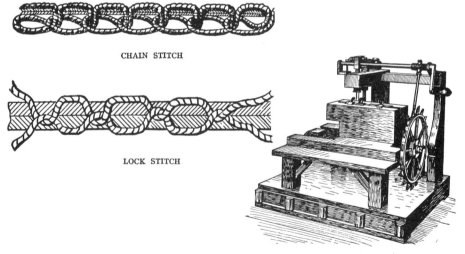

CHAIN STITCH

LOCK STITCH

THOMAS SAINT'S MACHINE OF 1790

146

sewed. The machine had an awl, to punch a hole in the goods. A needle, blunt and notched at the end, pushed a thread through the hole to form a loop on the under side of the material. Through this loop the needle, on next descending, passed a second loop to form a chain or crochet stitch. There was also a feed to move the goods along under the needle, a continuous thread, and stitch tighteners.

It is probable that by the time Saint finished his machine and secured his patent, he was too discouraged to go on with it. It may be, too, that to make a living he had to take up other work, and before he got back to his invention, he became sick and died. Whatever the reason, for almost sixty years his machine lay unknown in the English patent office. The result was that scores of would-be inventors worked on sewing machines, only to miss the good points in his invention. When it was finally brought to light, people looked at Saint's machine with amazement, and wondered how so great an invention could have been so completely forgotten.

The chain stitch made by Saint's machine had one drawback. When a break in the thread is followed by a slight pull, the chain stitch unravels. This does not occur with the lock stitch. The lock stitch is made by two threads. These are interlaced in the middle of the fabric sewn, so as to form a neat stitch on both sides of the fabric.

The first sewing machine to make a lock stitch was invented by Walter Hunt, of New York, about 1832. His machine had a curved needle with an eye at the point. The needle pierced the goods, and at the moment when it started out, a loop was formed in the thread. At that very same instant, a shuttle carrying a second thread passed through the loop, making the lock stitch.

Hunt was a gifted inventor. But either he thought little of his sewing machine, or he had other inventions that he thought promised greater and quicker profits. At any rate, he did not take the trouble to patent his machine, and proceeded to sell the model to a blacksmith for one hundred dollars. Even the blacksmith, after he had bought and paid for the model, made no use of it. Some twenty years afterward, when Howe's lock stitch machine became famous, this old discarded model was dug out of a rubbish heap, and application was entered for a patent. The patent was denied. Hunt, like Trevithick before him, just failed to win one of the big industrial prizes of the century.

Making His First Sewing Machine

It is often said that great inventions are a growth. This is true only when the would-be inventor makes use of what others before him have done. The idea of a sewing machine was not only new to Howe, but he did not know until many years afterward that Saint, or Hunt, or any one of a score of others in England, France, and America had ever made a sewing machine. So far as Howe knew, he was the first one in all the world who set out to make such a machine. So instead of trying to improve on what others before him had done, he went to work and created a new kind of machine altogether. For this reason, Howe's first sewing machine cannot be called a prototype.

When Howe first got the idea of inventing a sewing machine, he probably did a lot of thinking during his leisure hours about how such a machine could be made. But to take his regular turn at Ari Davis's shop called for all the strength he had. It was not long before he gave up active work on his invention, saying to himself, "Some day, I will invent a sewing machine." This became Howe's daydream.

But it was not to remain a daydream. In 1840 Howe married, and in time three children were born. His wages were only nine dollars a week. Nine dollars a week was

HOWE WATCHING HIS WIFE SEW

all too little to house, feed, and clothe a family of five. Besides, Howe's work was so hard that he often came home too tired to eat. He would go to bed, longing to lie there "forever and forever." Moved to act by the pinch of poverty, he began to think again about the machine which he had heard four years before would bring to its inventor a fortune. Then it was, about 1843, that the inventor's mania seized him, and gave him neither rest nor peace until he had made a sewing machine.

For almost a year, working evenings, Howe tried to make a machine that would imitate the motions of his wife's hands when sewing, and make a stitch such as she made. Every attempt to do this failed. One evening in the autumn of 1844, Howe sat thinking about his last attempt when there flashed into his mind this question: "Could there be another stitch that would do just as well as the stitch made by hand?" This question set Howe on a new track. He was familiar with the chain or crochet stitch, from often watching his wife sew. From working in machine shops, he also knew about shuttles and looms.

Soon he had an idea. It was short work to snap the point off of one of his wife's sewing needles and sharpen the head, thus making a needle with an eye at the point. With this he thrust the thread through two pieces of cloth to make a loop. With another needle he passed a second thread through the loop, and gently pulled the two threads to tighten the stitch. A half dozen lock stitches were thus quickly made. But would such stitches hold? Howe was so anxious he scarcely had courage to find out. He tried to pull the pieces of cloth apart, and found to his great relief that this new kind of stitch held even tighter than the common hand stitch.

It was easy enough to see how to make a machine to sew such stitches. But Howe lacked money to buy the materials, and had no money to support his family while making the model, which, if it was to be successful, must be made with as much care as a clock.

There lived at this time at Cambridge, an old friend and schoolmate of Howe's by the name of George Fisher. He had shortly before this time inherited a little money. Howe interested him in the invention. Fisher promised, for a half interest, to board Howe's family while he was making the machine, and to advance five hundred dollars for tools and materials. Fisher said afterward: "I was the

THE FIRST HOWE SEWING MACHINE

only one of his neighbors and friends . . . who had any confidence in the success of the invention. Howe was looked upon as very visionary in undertaking anything of the kind, and I was thought very foolish in helping him."

Throughout the winter of 1845, Howe toiled. He had the machine he wanted to make so vividly in mind that he worked almost as if he had a model before him. By May the first machine was complete. In July he did with it all the sewing on two suits of woolen clothes, one suit for himself and one for Mr. Fisher.

Howe's model was a strange-looking sewing machine. Every part has been improved, and many new ones have been added, but every one of the millions of sewing machines made since, owes at least one essential part to this machine, built in 1845. The way it sews is simple enough. The curved needle, with an eye at the point, carries the thread through the cloth, and the loop of the needle thread is locked by a thread passed through this loop by the shuttle. The materials are hung on the pins of the baster plate, which carries the goods along in front of the needle. The baster plate was the weakest part of the machine. The seam that could be made without stopping was short, and only straight seams could be sewed.

Exhibiting the Machine

As soon as the model was complete, Howe carried it to one of the clothing shops of Cambridge. He offered to sew any kind of garment brought to him. The incredulous tailors and seamstresses brought shirts, waists, skirts, and trousers, and were amazed to see the seams sewed perfectly, at the rate of two hundred and fifty stitches a minute, which is about seven times as fast as handwork. For two whole weeks, he sewed seams for all comers.

Finally he challenged five of the fastest seamstresses in the shop to a sewing contest. Ten seams of equal length were laid out. One seam was given to each of the five seamstresses and five seams to Howe. Howe was through first, and besides, the tailor who judged the contest, said that the work done on the machine was the neatest and the strongest.

One might suppose that Howe would at once have been flooded with requests for machines. But not one tailor, nor a single individual customer, came forward with an order.

Nor did Fisher and Howe have any better success at Washington, in the summer of 1846, where they went to take a model and secure a patent. While there, they exhibited the machine at a fair. They had an enjoyable time and heard "Ah's!" and "Oh's!" on all sides, but not one voice was heard by their anxious ears, asking to buy or even to rent a machine.

Fisher was now discouraged. The machine had been known to the public for more than a year, and not a single one had been sold. He had boarded Howe and his family for almost two years, besides advancing in all about two thousand dollars.

"I lost confidence," said Fisher, "in the machine's ever paying anything."

Offering the Machine to England

Howe was not to give up so easily. Borrowing money from his father, he sent his brother Amasa to England, to see what could be done there. The first man to buy one of Howe's machines was William Thomas, of London. Thomas had a large factory in which he made corsets, carpetbags, and shoes. Seeing the value of the machine for his business, he bought the one Amasa had with him, for twelve hundred and fifty dollars. This was a poor bargain, because it also included the right to use as many other machines as Thomas might need. Thomas was to

HOWE'S MODEL OF THE
SEWING-MACHINE.

The Wilson sewing machine of 1850

get also an English patent on the invention, promising to pay the inventor a royalty of fifteen dollars on each machine sold in England. Thomas patented the invention, but later refused to pay the promised royalty. By his foresight, along with his dishonesty, Thomas probably made on his investment of twelve hundred and fifty dollars, a net profit of a million dollars.

Howe still saw no prospect of making anything in America. When Thomas offered him fifteen dollars a week if he would go to England and adapt his machine to corset making and the like, he accepted. He set sail early in 1847, going in the steerage and cooking his own food. A little later he sent for his wife and children. For some eight months Howe worked to adjust his machine to the needs of Thomas's business. During all this time, Thomas treated him with respect. But when the work was done, Thomas made it so unpleasant that Howe had to give up his position. This left him a stranger in London, without work, and with a sick wife and three children to care for.

He had little money, but he undertook to make a fourth machine, hoping against hope that he could sell it at a good price. From Charles Inglis, a coachmaker, Howe rented a small shop, and with such tools as he could borrow, went to work. Long before the machine was finished, his money ran low. To reduce expenses, he moved his family from a three-room apartment to one room, and this in the poorest section of London. Fearful that he might not be able to get his family back to America, he decided to send them while he still had the money, trusting that he could follow when the machine was finished and sold.

"Before his wife left London," said Inglis, who proved a friend in time of need, "Howe had frequently borrowed money from me in sums of twenty-five dollars, and requested me to get him credit for provisions. On the evening of Mrs. Howe's departure, the night was very wet and stormy, and her health being delicate she was unable to walk to the ship. He lacked money to pay cab hire, and he borrowed it from me. He repaid it by pawning some of his clothing." Alone and without money, Howe had scarcely enough to eat to keep him alive. "He has borrowed a quarter from me," says Inglis, "for the

purpose of buying beans, which I saw him cook and eat in his own room."

The finished machine was worth at the very least two hundred and fifty dollars. But the only customer Howe could find was a workman, who offered him twenty-five dollars, providing he could have time in which to pay it. No one else wanting the machine at any price, Howe was obliged to accept this offer. The purchaser gave his note for twenty-five dollars, and Inglis succeeded in selling the note to another workman for twenty dollars. The small sum of twenty dollars was thus Howe's return for some four or five months of toil and humiliation. To pay his debts and secure passage home, he was compelled to pawn his precious first machine and his letters of patent. Even then he had so little money that, to save cartage, he borrowed a handcart and hauled his own baggage to the ship.

Howe landed at New York in April 1849. Four years had come and gone since the completion of the first machine. The one lone fifty-cent piece in his pocket was the only visible reward for these years of anxiety and toil. Yet Howe was happy. He heard that there was plenty of work in New York, and within a few hours he had a position as a mechanic in a machine shop.

A few days after this, news came that his wife was dying of a strange disease. He had no money to make the trip to Cambridge and could not go until his father — ever loyal — sent him the needed ten dollars. Howe arrived at his wife's bedside just in time to see her alive. The only clothes he had were the working clothes he wore, and to appear at her funeral he borrowed a suit from his brother-in-law.

Under such trials and humiliations Howe aged rapidly, and he looked like a man who had been through a severe illness. But he was once more among friends. They did not think much of his invention, but they loved the man. His children were being cared for, and soon he was hard at work again, not on his machine, but as a mechanic at a regular wage.

Fighting for His Rights

If money was not to be made out of the sewing machine as a useful invention, there were persons who thought that money could be made out of it as a curiosity. On the streets of Ithaca, New York, in May 1849, you might have seen this show bill:

A GREAT
CURIOSITY
THE YANKEE SEWING MACHINE
IS NOW
EXHIBITING
AT THIS PLACE
FROM
8 A.M. TO 5 P.M.

People came in numbers to see the new wonder, and women carried home samples of sewing as souvenirs.

LADIES OF ITHACA IN 1849, WATCHING THE SEWING MACHINE AT WORK

SINGER WORKING AT HIS FIRST MACHINE

This advertising led a few persons to want machines. Mechanics, especially in Boston, began to make and sell them. But this was not all. Other inventors entered the field. Among these was Isaac M. Singer, who added many practical parts and who did much to bring the sewing machine before the public.

Singer's interest in the sewing machine was aroused in the summer of 1850, while on a business trip to Boston. In the shop of a Mr. Phelps he saw a crude machine patterned after Howe's model at Washington. Noting Singer's interest, Phelps remarked: "If the sewing machine could be made to do a greater variety of work, it would be a good thing." Howe's machine, you know, sewed only a straight seam.

During the evening, at his hotel, Singer worked out the

drawings for several changes. The next morning he showed a rough sketch of the proposed machine to Phelps and to a Mr. Zieber. They were satisfied that it would work. But Singer had no money to make a machine. Zieber proposed to advance forty dollars for the purpose, and Phelps offered to make the model in his shop. Work on the model started that very day.

"I worked at it day and night," said Singer long afterward, "sleeping but three or four hours out of the twenty-four, and eating generally but once a day, as I knew I must make it for the forty dollars, or not get it at all.

"The machine was completed in eleven days. At about nine o'clock in the evening we got the parts together, and tried it. It did not sew. The workmen, exhausted with almost constant work, pronounced it a failure, and left me, one by one.

"Zieber held the lamp, and I continued to try the machine, but anxiety and incessant work had made me nervous, and I could not get tight stitches. Sick at heart, at about midnight we started for our hotel. On the way, we sat down on a pile of boards, and Zieber mentioned that the loose loops of thread were on the upper side of the cloth. It flashed upon me that we had forgotten to adjust the tension on the needle thread. We went back, adjusted the tension, tried the machine, sewed five stitches perfectly, and the thread snapped. But that was enough."

Thus in the course of eleven days, Singer, working at great speed, improved Howe's machine and added new features. Among these are the overhanging arms, the spring foot near the needle, and the double-acting treadle. By 1851, he had his machine ready for the market.

If Mr. Singer was not a great inventor, he was skillful in making practical the ideas of others, and he was a great business man. He more than anyone else, aroused the world to the value of the sewing machine. He did this through advertising. He used posters, pamphlets, almanacs, and newspapers, to tell of the worth of the new invention. Sewing machine shows were held in towns and cities; there were bands to attract the people, and skillful young ladies to exhibit the wonderful work of the new marvel. Sewing contests were arranged, and prizes were given to the speediest and best sewers. Local agents were employed, and these agents, with their wagons loaded with machines, went everywhere. No wonder that a man as modern in his methods as Singer made a fortune, and that he was the founder of the greatest sewing machine company in the world today.

To return to Howe: As Howe worked away at a

mechanic's wage, he learned that sewing machines were being exhibited in different parts of the country as curiosities, and that persons were making and selling them. He examined some of these, and found that they were either made after his model at Washington, or embodied the essential parts of his machine. But never a word was said about his being the inventor. To secure his rights, as well as the reward for his labor, nothing remained but to take the matter to the courts.

Howe lacked means, but he succeeded in interesting a man of wealth, who bought Mr. Fisher's half interest in the patent, and also advanced money to prosecute the infringers. The new partner, however, did not want to lose any money on the venture. To protect himself against loss, he demanded a mortgage on the farm of Howe's father. The father, faithful to the end, consented. Suits in court, then as now, went forward slowly, and Howe had time for other things. We find him in New York in 1850, making and selling fourteen of his machines. A few of those who had also been making and selling machines, fearful of the consequences, secured licenses from Howe, and this added a little to his income.

But Howe was busy chiefly, during the years 1850-1854, with his different cases in the courts. Singer, the chief infringer, contested Howe's rights the hardest. To show that Howe was not the inventor of the sewing machine, the inventions of Saint, Hunt, and many others were brought into court. Finally in 1854, a verdict was rendered which gave Howe the victory. The judge found Howe's patent valid, and declared; "There is no evidence . . . that leaves the shadow of a doubt, that, for all the benefits conferred on the public by the invention of the sewing machine, the public is indebted to Mr. Howe."

Reaping the Reward

Meanwhile, the new partner had died. His heirs, having no faith in the future of the sewing machine, sold their share to Howe at a low price. For the first time he was the sole owner of his invention. The mercy of God was at last on his side. The public began to appreciate the sewing machine and suddenly a great demand arose for them. Howe received a royalty on each kind of sewing machine made in the United States, no matter where they were sold. A perfect flood of gold soon poured in upon him. In a very few years his income leaped from three hundred dollars to two hundred thousand dollars a year. In all he received about two million dollars in royalties, or approximately a hundred thousand a year, for the twenty years of his life devoted to his invention.

In return for this he gave an invention, which, as it has

improved, has lessened the work and added to the comfort of almost every home in the civilized world. Sewing machines are today found alike in the jungles of the Amazon, and on the heights of the Himalayas. His invention has given birth also to new industries, such as the making of ready-made clothing. So enormous has this business become that single factories using hundreds of power machines, and employing thousands of women, turn out but one kind of article, such as dresses for girls or suits for boys. And it has given new life to more than fifty old trades, such as the making of straw hats, shoes, and dresses. Even the manufacture and sale of sewing machines has in itself become a giant industry. If Howe's reward for his toil and anxiety was great, great also was his gift to the world.

Comprehension Questions

1. What two inventors came out with sewing machines before Mr. Howe?
2. Who was George Fisher?
3. Was William Thomas willing to deal fairly and justly with Mr. Howe?
4. What were some of the improvements that Mr. Singer made to the sewing machine?
5. How did Elias Howe finally manage to gain the rights to the sewing machine?

Chapter 8

Cyrus H. McCormick and the Invention of the Reaper

The most vital occupation the world over is farming, because our food comes from the farm. The most important article of food is bread, and the best bread is made from wheat. The amount of wheat raised depends largely on the amount that can be harvested. The farmer, as a rule, has ample time to prepare the ground and sow the wheat, but the time within which he can harvest the golden grain is limited to from four to ten days. Very soon after the wheat ripens, the stalks begin to break and fall down, and the grain begins to shatter. Unless cut very soon after it is ripe, the crop is lost. The harvesting of wheat is, then, most important. Each improvement in methods of harvesting has increased the amount of wheat raised, and has decreased the amount of hunger in the world.

The Sickle and the Cradle

In the very earliest times, the harvester walked along and pulled the heads off by hand, leaving the stalks to stand in the field. The first improvement over this primitive method was the use of a long-bladed knife. By grasping some stalks with one hand, and using the knife with the other, many heads could be cut off at one stroke. A knife that was slightly curved worked better than one with a straight blade, and this led to the making of the sickle.

In the days when the sickle was king, the whole family turned out to help gather in the harvest. The women could reap as well as the men. It was a good day's work for one person to cut and bind into sheaves or bundles a half acre of wheat. This would yield anywhere from five to twenty bushels of grain.

HARVESTING WITH THE SICKLE IN COLONIAL DAYS

170

Cyrus H. McCormick and the Reaper

HARVESTING WITH THE CRADLE

The sickle gave way to the cradle, which first came into use about the time of the Revolutionary War. The cradle is merely a scythe furnished with wooden fingers running parallel with the blade. These wooden fingers hold the stalks of grain, after they have been cut off, in an upright position, and enable the cradler to lay the grain down in a neat row, with the stalks parallel, ready to be gathered into bunches and bound into sheaves.

A strong man could cut with a cradle from two to two-

171

and-a-half acres of wheat in a day. A second man following along could gather it up and bind it into sheaves. The cradle was thus a great improvement over the sickle or reap hook, for it increased two to three times the amount of wheat one man could harvest. But cradling and binding grain was the very hardest work on the farm. In hot weather even the strongest men could keep at work only a part of the time. So long, then, as the cradle was the best means of harvesting, the amount of wheat that could be raised on a single farm was small. Still, the cradle continued to be the king of harvesters until almost the middle of the nineteenth century. Even today, wheat raised in stumpy ground, in small fields, and in orchards, is cut with a cradle.

BELL'S REAPER AT WORK

The First Reaping Machines

The success of men like Watt with the steam engine, and Arkwright with the water frame, encouraged many a man in England to work on labor-saving machines. One of these, Patrick Bell of Scotland, came close to making a practical reaper.

The important point to be noticed about Bell's reaper is the cutting apparatus. It is made up of twelve pairs of shears or scissors. One side of each pair of shears is fastened to the cutter bar and stands still. The other side is fastened on a pivot and vibrates back and forth and thus cuts the grain. The reel draws the grain against the blades of the scissors, and causes the cut grain to fall upon a moving canvas. The moving canvas carries the grain to one side, out of the way of the horses, which are hitched behind the machine. In workmanship, this machine was far ahead of any reaper made in America until at least 1847. Bell's reaper was first tried in the harvest of 1828, and a public exhibition of its work was given in that year.

"This reaper," said a writer in 1852, "soon worked its way to a considerable success . . . In the harvest of 1834 I saw several of them at work, all giving satisfaction. They were manufactured in England, and eventually found their way throughout the country. Four of them went to the United States of America. This renders it highly probable that they became the models from which the many so-called inventions of the American reapers have since sprung. . . . In a few cases the Bell reaper has kept in operation up to the present time."

Why, then, did this machine not come into general use, and why is Bell not called the inventor of the reaper? The cutting part of Bell's machine, as in all the early reapers, was not satisfactory. If the grain was ripe, stood up well, and was free from grass and weeds, it went satisfactorily. But if the grain was down, and there was an abundance of weeds and grass, the machine choked, running over the wheat without cutting it. As a rule, only about four-fifths of a field could be harvested with this machine; the remainder had to be cut with the cradle. Again, farmers were not accustomed at that time to machinery. Besides, the fields in England were small, and labor was plentiful. English farmers did not have much trouble in harvesting what grain they could raise. There was not, for these reasons, very much encouragement in England for an inventor to make the sacrifice to perfect a machine and to educate the people to buy and use it. Still, if Bell is not to be called the inventor of the reaper, it should be granted that he made the first reaping machine used to any considerable extent.

The Man Who Succeeded

Although Bell's reaper cut grain with some success, people went on harvesting their wheat with the sickle and cradle, almost as if his invention had not been made. But not long afterward, a reaper was invented which, when perfected, was used in all parts of the world. This reaper replaced the sickle and the cradle; it increased, many times, the amount of wheat raised, and it relieved the farmers of the back-breaking work of cutting and binding grain by hand. The man who took the chief part in the invention and improvement of this reaper was an American, Cyrus H. McCormick, born in 1809, near Midvale, Virginia.

Robert McCormick, the father of Cyrus, was a farmer, who, like many other farmers of the day, did other things besides farming. On his large farm of 1800 acres, there stood a sawmill and a gristmill. There was also a large blacksmith shop where the father not only made and repaired the tools used on the farm, but often tried his hand at invention. A reaping machine was his hobby. He was at work on this as early as 1816, and continued to busy himself with it until 1831. At the time it left his hands, the cutting part was made up of whirling saws eight to ten inches in diameter, which revolved like shears past the edge of stationary knives. A reel pressed the grain against the cutters, and pushed the cut grain upon a platform. When there was enough cut grain on the platform to make a sheaf, it was raked to the ground by a man who followed along beside the reaper. This machine was at last tested in the early harvest of 1831, but the cutter would not work.

Cyrus H. McCormick, the oldest of a family of eight children, grew up like any other country boy, familiar from childhood with farm life. He prided himself on knowing how to do every kind of farm work, and how to run and repair every bit of machinery in use. The winter months he spent in the nearby "Field School," studying reading, writing, and arithmetic. The rest of the year he was expected to work, either on the farm, in the mills, or in the shop. When he was twenty-one, Cyrus was as big and strong as any man in all the region round about; he was a good farmer, and was skilled in the use of blacksmith tools. Like his father, he had a fondness for making things and for invention.

McCormick's First Reaper

When Robert McCormick, the father of Cyrus, drew his crude reaper out to a field of wheat in the early harvest of 1831, to make a trial of the invention on which he had spent fifteen years, Cyrus was more than an onlooker. He had a considerable part in the making of this machine. So when it choked down and would not cut, he was probably even more disappointed than his father. But when the disappointed father said, "I am through with it; it is impossible to make a practical reaping machine," Cyrus did not give up. The surrender of the father was the call of the son to battle. Then and there Cyrus resolved to make a successful reaper. The machine was pulled back to the blacksmith shop, and Cyrus took up the work where his father left off.

To improve the cutting part of the machine, Cyrus made a sickle bar, to carry a moving sickle, with wire guards extending forward into the grain. The sickle was made of a thin bar of steel, on the edge of which were filed sharp, saw-like teeth. A divider was attached to the outer end of the sickle bar, and extended forward, to separate the grain to be cut from the grain to be left standing. These two changes were probably the only ones made on his father's machine in the summer of 1831. Cyrus was anxious to give the new kind of cutter a trial. So before the last oats were cut, the improved machine was taken back to the field. The new cutter worked so well that Cyrus felt he was on the right track.

By the harvest of 1832, the improved machine probably

McCORMICK'S MACHINE, 1831–1834, CUTTING A FIELD OF OATS

looked very much like the machine patented in 1834. Cyrus felt ready to take his machine out into the "wide, wide world." A public exhibition was given near Lexington, which was attended by the farmers and laborers for miles around. The field in which the trial was to be made was very rough. The machine did not work well, and it looked for a time as if it also were a failure.

"Here," shouted the owner of the field, "stop your horses.

178

Cyrus H. McCormick and the Reaper

That won't do, you are ruining my wheat."

This delighted the laborers, who feared that the machine would take work away from them.

"It's a humbug," shouted one.

"Give me the old cradle yet," cried another.

All this, you may be sure, was discouraging enough to the farmer-inventor. But farmers like fair play.

"I'll see that you have a fair chance, young man," said a farmer. "That field of wheat on the other side of the fence belongs to me. Pull down the fence and cross over."

Cyrus pulled down the fence and crossed over. The field was level, and before sundown he had laid low a full six acres of grain.

With this unheard-of feat accomplished, the machine was driven into Lexington and exhibited at the courthouse square. One spectator, after looking it over carefully, said, "This machine is worth a hundred thousand dollars."

Probably as agreeable to Cyrus were the words of his father: "It makes me feel proud, to have a son do what I could not do."

The general feeling of most of those who saw the machine on that day was, however, probably expressed by a certain lady, who said, "I thought it was a right smart curious sort of a thing, but that it wouldn't come to much."

Selling Reapers In the East

McCormick advertised reapers for sale in the local newspaper as early as 1833. But it was seven years before he sold his first machine. To be sure, between 1833 and 1839 he was engaged with his father in running an iron furnace, and gave little time to his invention. The iron business, however, proved a failure, McCormick losing everything. The reaper was all he had left. He now turned to it to help him out of his financial troubles, exhibiting it in the harvest of 1839. Through he cut as much as twelve acres of grain in a day, no one wanted to buy. To the farmers of that time the machine was not only costly — the price was fifty dollars — but it was also very complex. "It can be run," said the farmers, "right well, by one who knows all its cogs and levers, but we are running farms and not circuses."

Most persons would have been discouraged, and have given up. McCormick was not that kind of man; he worked even harder than before. He succeeded in selling seven machines in 1842, twenty-nine in 1843, and fifty in 1844. This was big business.

Best of all, seven reapers were ordered from the West. These seven orders gave great joy to the McCormick brothers, who were now all busy at the old blacksmith shop, turning out a reaper a week. But when the question of how to deliver reapers out to Ohio, Missouri, Iowa, Illinois, and Wisconsin arose, Cyrus saw that the old "home farm" was no place to make reapers, if these were to be sent to the West.

About this time a friend remarked, "Cyrus, why don't you go West with your reaper, where the fields are large and level, and where labor is scarce?"

McCormick decided that this was the best thing for him to do. In a few days he was on his way. He traveled by stage through Pennsylvania, by boat along the lake ports, and on horseback over the Middle Western States. It was the first time he had seen the prairies, so broad and level and fertile. They seemed made for his reaper, and in Illinois he realized how greatly the West needed it. The bounteous harvest was too much to be cut with the cradle, and hogs and cattle had been turned into great fields of over-ripe grain.

"With my reaper," thought McCormick, "millions of bushels of grain can be saved, which are now left to rot on the ground. Here and there in Virginia, a farmer can be persuaded by hard work to buy a reaper, but the West — the West must have the reaper."

Chicago in 1832

Reaping-Machine, or Harvester.

Cyrus H. McCormick and the Reaper

Carrying the Reaper to the West

Returning home, McCormick brought together all the improvements he had made in his machine since his first patent, and took out a new one in 1845.

He was going West, but where should he locate? St. Louis, Detroit, Cincinnati, and Cleveland were cities of good size, and each offered some special advantage. But McCormick studied the maps, saw where the railroads were going, and observed where the people were settling. He finally chose Chicago. This was one of the best decisions in his long and successful career.

When McCormick voted for Chicago, he had neither money nor credit. To start in business, he must find a man to furnish him with the needed money. McCormick called on William Ogden, then Mayor of Chicago, and told him of his invention, of his success, and of his new plans. On hearing McCormick's story, Ogden said, "You are just the man we want. I will give you twenty-five thousand dollars for half-interest in this reaper business of yours, and we will build a factory at once." The factory was built, and five hundred reapers were manufactured for the harvest of 1848, and fifteen hundred for the harvest of the next year. The making of reapers on a large scale in the West was thus a success from the first.

After the second year, McCormick said to Ogden, "For your share of the business, I will pay you back the twenty-five thousand dollars you invested, and will give you twenty-five thousand besides for interest and profit."

Ogden, having many other interests, gladly accepted this offer; he had doubled his money in two years. McCormick now had a factory of his own, and the commanding position of being the inventor and successful maker of the reaper. He was well on the way to a great fortune. From this time on, he had no partners except his brothers, who joined him in Chicago, to help in the growing business.

The Self-Rake Reaper

The reaper did away with the hard work of cutting grain with the sickle or cradle. Farmers soon began to ask, "Why cannot a device be invented to do away with the even harder work of the raker?" In answer, a self-rake was invented in 1852, by Jearum Atkins, an invalid. Atkins had a McCormick reaper placed outside his window. Day after day he sat in his chair and worked on an attachment which would of itself rake from the platform the cut grain. Success finally crowned his efforts, and McCormick, always anxious to meet the demands of the farmer, bought this invention.

The farmers nicknamed the contrivance the "Iron Man." It was surely a spectacle to see its long, rake-fingered arm whirling up through the air, and then, descending to the platform, rake off the cut grain in great bunches ready to be bound. The automatic rake saved the labor of one to two men, and after 1860 farmers rarely bought any other kind of machine.

McCORMICK SELF-RAKE REAPER

185

The Marsh Harvester

The reaper by this time had taken away fully half the hard work of the harvest. There remained only the binding of the bunches of cut grain around the middle with a straw rope, so that the grain could be easily handled. This, to be sure, was back-breaking toil, but most of the farmers thought it would always have to be done by hand. "How can a machine ever gather the grain into bundles and tie bands about them?" they would ask.

An inventor by the name of Mann fitted a McCormick reaper, in 1849, with a canvas elevator. This carried the cut grain up into a wagon moving along beside the machine. Nine years later, two brothers by the name of Marsh were using a machine of this kind, when one asked the other, "Why should the grain be carried up to the wagon? Why can't we put a platform on the side of the machine to stand on, make a table all round to work on, and bind the grain as fast as it comes up?"

By the next harvest, the Marsh boys had their new rigging arranged. As they expected, they could bind grain nearly three times as fast as before. One of the brothers bound a whole acre by himself, in fifty-five minutes. They patented their device, and called it the Marsh harvester.

The Marsh harvester cut the cost of binding grain in half. The workers no longer had to walk from bundle to bundle, nor were they compelled to stoop over each time they bound a sheaf. They could stand still and straight at their work. Two men could do what before it took five or six to do. Strange as it may seem, the Marsh harvester was not at first popular. The farmers called it a "man killer." The farm hands dubbed it the "Weary Willie." Like all good things, it soon won its way, and for more than ten years was the king of harvesters.

Besides reducing the cost and the drudgery of binding grain, the Marsh harvester was a long step toward what the farmers had said could never be done. All that was now needed to do "the impossible" was to teach the Marsh harvester to twist a wire or to tie a knot.

The Wire Self-Binder

In the winter of 1874, Charles Withington, of Janesville, Wisconsin, carried to McCormick at Chicago a new invention. It was a remarkable device. Two steel arms caught a bundle of grain between them, put a wire tightly around the bundle, and fastened the two ends of the wire together by a twist. This was the long-sought self-binder, the very thing the farmers said could never be made. A wire self-binder was built and tested in the following July.

It cut fifty acres of wheat, and bound almost every bundle without a slip. Within the next five years, McCormick alone made and sold fifty thousand of these machines.

This was the end of harvest drudgery. Sickles, cradles, rakers, binders, each in turn were set free. From this time on, all that was needed was a man or a good-sized boy to drive the team and to manage the machine. The machine cut the grain, bound it into sheaves, collected these on a carrier, and dropped them to the ground, ready to be placed in shocks — all without the aid of the human hand.

THE WIRE SELF-BINDER

The Twine Self-Binder

There was one defect in the wire binder, which proved to be its undoing. The wire mixed with the straw and got into the mouths of the cattle, and at times killed them. Pieces of wire mixed in the grain cut the hands of those handling it. So, while the farmers were delighted with the self-binder, they disliked the wire.

At the very time the wire binder seemed the best hope for the harvester world, John Appleby, of Wisconsin, took to William Deering, the chief maker of the Marsh harvester, an invention which he claimed could tie a knot more quickly and more securely than was ever done by sailor.

Deering knew the dislike of the farmers for wire.

"Here," he said to himself, "is the device to make the perfect binder, a binder that will use twine." He immediately accepted the new device without the slightest hesitation.

During the winter of 1880, word went about among the makers of binders that "Deering is crazy over a twine binder. Why, he is making three thousand of them."

Before the harvest of 1880 was over, the shoe was on the other foot. Deering not only made, but he sold his three thousand twine binders, at a profit of one hundred thousand dollars.

By the next harvest almost every manufacturer was in the field with a twine binder, most of them paying a royalty to Appleby. The wire binder passed away almost as quickly as a summer shower. The twine binder took its place, and it is today the standard binder of the world. It is the free exchange of goods and services known as "free enterprise" that has given the American people many new and improved inventions.

With one of these machines, a sixteen-year-old boy can harvest as much grain as a dozen strong men could harvest with the cradle. Modern reapers with gasoline engines, known as combines, can run even faster and stronger than the horse-drawn harvesters designed by McCormick. These new tractors can harvest, thresh and clean a field of oats or wheat in record time. However, the modern grain combine is largely based upon the original design of Mr. McCormick.

The Worth of the Reaper

McCormick lived until 1884. He thus saw the reaper grow from the time he drove that crude machine back to the old blacksmith shop in July 1831, until it reached the point of being a highly successful farm machine. With his own hand, he added the improvements that first made the reaper a success. In his own time he was always the largest single maker of reapers, and he did more than anyone else to carry the reaper to Europe and to the other countries of the world.

Chiefly because of the reaper, the amount of wheat produced in the world has increased by leaps and bounds. It now amounts to several billions of bushels a year. To handle this enormous crop, great elevators are built along railroads, at railroad centers, and at seaports. To grind this wheat, thousands of flour mills have been built, some of which are so large that a single mill grinds seventeen thousand barrels of flour in twenty-four hours. Even the making of reapers became a great industry. One harvester company alone gives regular employment to an army of twenty-five thousand men and women.

Thank God that Cyrus McCormick had the freedom to "do the impossible!" The United States will remain strong as long as people have the opportunity to freely produce new goods and services.

Comprehension Questions

1. Describe why the cradle was an improvement over the sickle.
2. Who invented the first reaping machine to be used by the public?
3. What was the name of Cyrus McCormick's father?
4. What city was finally chosen by McCormick for his reaper factory in the west?
5. What problems eventually developed with the wire self-binder?
6. In what year did Cyrus McCormick die?

A MODERN HARVESTER

Chapter 9

Henry Bessemer and the Making of Steel

Iron is the most useful metal in the world. It is the most useful metal in the world, because it is the most helpful. Without iron to make our stoves, kettles, knives, tools, engines, and railroads, we would be living today very much as the Indians lived when Columbus discovered America. Our cooking utensils, our tools, and our weapons would, to this very day, be of clay or wood or stone. Pound for pound, pure gold is worth more than pure iron. But when it is made up into useful articles, iron may be worth more than a

HENRY BESSEMER

corresponding weight of gold. For example, a bar of iron worth five dollars, is worth seventy-five dollars when made into needles and three thousand dollars when made into razor blades.

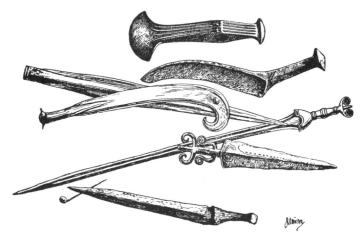

IMPLEMENTS OF THE BRONZE AGE

Primitive Iron Furnaces

Most of the countries of the world have at least some iron ore. Yet people mixed copper and tin to form bronze, and fashioned bronze tools and weapons long before they learned to use iron. The reason for this was that iron is not found by itself, like gold, copper, or tin. It is mixed with clay, or rock, or other substances, and in this form is called iron ore. To obtain the iron, the ore must be put under great heat. When this is done, the iron in the ore melts and runs out, and only then can it be collected and made into useful things.

The first furnace in which iron ore was melted was probably no more than a pile of wood with a layer of ore on top. The entire heap was covered with clay to keep in the heat.

PRIMITIVE FORGE IN NORTHERN EUROPE, 1600

A large hole at the top and several holes at the bottom provided the needed draft. The reward for several days' work with such a furnace was a couple of pounds of iron. Yet the smith forged from the iron obtained in this way, crude knives, axes, and spearheads that were superior to similar tools and weapons made of stone or of bronze.

CHARCOAL PIT

In the course of time, improvements were made on this method of smelting iron. Charred wood, or charcoal, which makes a hotter fire, came to be used instead of wood. A goatskin bellows was added to fan the fire. With a bellows to force the air into the furnace, the draft could be made stronger than when the air entered of its own accord. More importantly, the draft could be controlled. The furnace was then built so that it could be used again. It was made of clay, and at least one form was four or five feet high and about five feet wide at the bottom. An opening was left in front, which was closed with clay after the furnace was filled with layers of charcoal and iron ore, and was broken down after each melting, so that the melted iron could be taken out.

One of these improved furnaces would supply from fifteen to twenty pounds of iron in a day. There was at last, iron enough for knives, axes, spears, swords, chisels, saws, files, forks, weapons, and chains. When these improvements in the furnace were brought about no one knows, but they were all probably made long before the Israelites were in bondage in Egypt.

For more than two thousand years after this, there was little progress in smelting iron. What there was, consisted in building better furnaces, and in making them so that the charcoal and the iron ore could be put in at the top, and the smelted iron and the slag could be drawn off at the bottom. Such a furnace could be run for months, and even for years, without being allowed to cool down.

The Blast Furnace

About the time of Columbus, other improvements followed. Furnaces were built still larger, some of them as high as twenty or thirty feet. More powerful bellows also came into use, which were worked by horse power or by water power. These larger furnaces with the more powerful bellows, called blast furnaces, produced from two to three tons of iron a day.

The modern blast furnace dates, however, from the introduction of the steam engine. This did away with the bellows worked by horse power or water power, and made possible the use of blowers, which deliver a blast of air strong enough to blow a person off his feet.

Smelting iron required so much wood that countries like England became alarmed. It was feared that all the good timber would be burned up. A trial was made of soft coal, but it was not satisfactory. The custom of charring wood to make charcoal probably suggested the idea of charring soft coal, and using the coke, or charred coal. Coke answered very well for smelting iron, and its use became general in western Europe about 1750.

Up to 1828, cold air was used to fan the fire. Then an ingenious Englishman made a great discovery. He found that if the air was heated very hot before it was forced into the furnace, the iron could be smelted with half the amount of fuel otherwise required.

The forced blast, the hot blast, and the use of coke are thus the important features of the modern blast furnace. These modern furnaces are built from seventy-five to a hundred feet high, and from twenty to thirty feet wide inside at the widest part. A single blast furnace of average size will turn out a hundred tons of iron a day. It will produce as much iron as six to seven thousand of the furnaces of ancient times.

There is scarcely any limit to the amount of iron the modern blast furnace can produce. But the blast furnace has one drawback. The iron made in primitive furnaces could be hammered at once into tools and implements. Only the iron needed for knife blades, swords, and the like had to be refined, or changed into a finer kind of steel. The iron produced in a blast furnace, called pig iron, will not bend, and it cannot be hammered. It can be melted and molded into castings, such as stove tops and stove lids. But before it can be pressed or hammered into useful things, it has to be refined. To change pig iron into the higher grades of steel needed to make delicate machines and fine tools, such as knives, axes, saws, and chisels, was at this time very expensive.

The invention of the steam engine, the steamboat, the locomotive, the sewing machine, and the like, increased the amount of good steel that was needed. It seemed that the progress of the world was to be halted, unless some way was found to change the cheap pig iron, of which there was an abundance, into steel, at less expense. What the world needed was someone to do for the making of steel what Crompton had done for spinning, Whitney for cotton growing, and McCormick for wheat raising. The man to do this was born at Charlton, England, in 1813. His name was Henry Bessemer.

Preparing for Work

In 1813 Charlton was a small country village. There, among the woods and fields and country folk, Henry Bessemer lived. He received a good elementary school education, but he did not go to high school. Instead, he educated himself at home in the years between the ages of thirteen and sixteen. Some of the neighbors said he was fooling his time away. However that may be, he was fond of working on a lathe that his father bought for him. He made working models of machines. One of these was a brick machine, with which he molded little bricks of white clay. He also molded, in type metal, wheels, pulleys, and other objects. "Often during my evening walks around the fields, with a favorite dog," he says in his autobiography, "I would take up a small lump of yellow clay from the roadside, and fashion it into some grotesque head or material object, from which I would afterward make a mold and cast it in type metal."

Henry's father owned a big type foundry. This was a place of great interest. Many a day he spent there, cutting dies, molding type, and mixing different kinds of type metal. Though strictly forbidden, he often stole secretly into the melting house and watched the workmen make the type metal. But the antimony used in making the type

BESSEMER BUYING MEDALLIONS FROM A VENDER

metal caused Henry more than once to become sick, and his sickness finally betrayed him. As the Bible states so well, "Be sure that your sins will find you out."

"There was . . . one other attraction in the village, which played an important part in molding my ideas," he tells us. "I was very fond of machinery, and of watching it in motion. If ever I were absent from meals, I could probably have been found at the flour mill . . . where I passed many hours, gazing with pleasure upon the broad sheet of water falling into the . . . buckets of the great . . . water wheel; or, perhaps, I might have been watching, with a feeling almost of awe, the large wooden spur wheel, which brought up the speed, and which was one of the wonders of the millwright's craft in those days."

By the time Henry was seventeen years old, he was full grown, a little more than six feet tall, and full of energy. He was to become the Thomas Edison of England. But he did not begin to work with any big plan in mind, as to how he was going to become the most famous inventor of his age. He merely had wide-open eyes, and did the thing before him which seemed worth doing.

Making Art Castings and Stamping Dies

On one of his rambles about London, where his parents moved in 1830, young Bessemer met with an Italian selling plaster casts "of the most beautiful medallions, real works of art, at one penny apiece." He bought several of the most beautiful of the medallions and took them home, to cast them in metal. After working with the very greatest patience for more than a year, he not only succeeded in casting medallions in metal, but he perfected his way of casting. He was able to reproduce in metal, rosebuds, flowers, ferns, indeed any natural object, with all their delicate curves and fine lines. He also found a way of putting a coat of copper on his casts, so that they looked as if they were made of bronze.

His casts were really beautiful, and attracted attention even among artists. Thus by following out a boyish interest, and by putting to use the skill he had acquired, Bessemer was started on his great career. The neighbors, meanwhile, complained that the young man was allowed to fool his time away.

While busy with his art castings, his attention was called to the use of dies to stamp raised figures on cardboard and leather. It was a short step from making molds for casting medallions and flowers, to making dies for stamping raised figures. Then, too, Bessemer had made many a die at Charlton when "fooling his time away."

"After a certain amount of practice," he tells us, "I produced many very beautiful dies . . . I built a powerful 'fly-press' for stamping impressions from these dies.

"It will be easy to imagine my delight on securing my first order for five hundred copies, on . . . cardboard, of a beautiful cartoon of Raphael. These impressions cost me only three pence each . . . and I found ready sale for them at a half crown.

DESIGN OF BESSEMER'S DIE, 1833

"I also made many dies . . . for bookbinders, cardboard manufacturers, etc., thus turning to commercial account the art of 'fine casting,' which I had previously only pursued as an amusement."

Making a Stamp Die for the Government

While thus engaged, Bessemer learned that the government was being defrauded of probably five hundred thousand dollars a year. People were taking stamps from old and useless deeds, and using them on new deeds. Bessemer thought a stamp could be made that would prevent this fraud. Everything else was set aside and neglected, for this great object was to make his fortune. After some months, the die was completed. It was made of steel, and punched four hundred little holes in the parchment, each of them forming a part of the design of the stamp. The die was no sooner finished, than Bessemer was off to the president of the Stamp Office. In triumph he said to himself: "A few more weeks will seal the fate of my life. If I succeed in saving the government so much revenue, they must reward me liberally. I shall then establish myself in a new home, and marry the young lady to whom I have for two years been engaged.

"The design gave great satisfaction . . . and the Stamp Office authorities decided to adopt it. I was then asked if, instead of receiving a sum of money from the Treasury, I should be satisfied with the position of Superintendent of Stamps, at three or four thousand dollars a year. This was all I could want. . . . A few days after this . . . I called on the young lady to whom I was engaged, and showed her . . . my new . . . stamp. I explained to her how it could never be removed and used again . . . when she at once said, 'Yes I understand this; but surely, if all the stamps had a date upon them, they could not be used again without detection.' While I felt pleased and proud at the clever and simple suggestion of the young lady, I saw also that all my more elaborate system of piercing dies, the result of months of study, and the toil of many a weary and lonely night, was shattered to pieces by it."

Bessemer felt in honor bound to present to the authorities the new die with the movable dates. It was so simple that it was adopted and is in use even to this day. But the new die was so simple that there was no need of a superintendent of stamps at four thousand dollars a year. Bessemer thought, of course, that the government would pay him liberally for his nine months of labor. At first there were half-promises of reward. But the Stamp Office finally told him that he had offered the die to the government of his own free will, and that there was no money to give him. "Sad and dispirited, and with a burning sense of injustice overpowering all other feelings," he says, "I went my way from the Stamp Office, too proud to ask as a favor that which was . . . my just right."

This was a hard blow for a young man who thought he all

but had a good position for life, and could marry at once the girl he loved. He was, however, not altogether discouraged. "I have made one good invention," he said to himself, "and I can make others. I will keep my eyes open for a 'good vein,' and when I find it, I will work it for all it is worth." For the next four or five years, he was busy with several inventions, when by accident he discovered the first of the "good veins" he was to find.

Making Bronze Powder

Henry's sister asked him one day to letter the title and her name on the cover of a flower book. The book was so beautiful that Henry thought common ink would not look good enough. He decided to do the letters in a paint made of bronze powder, so that they would look as if they were made in gold. When he went to get the bronze

BESSEMER LETTERING HIS SISTER'S
ALBUM

206

powder, he was astonished to learn that a little ounce bottle cost a dollar and a half. Most of us would have grumbled at the price, then paid it, and gone our way. Not so with Bessemer; his eyes were wide open for a "good vein."

"On my way home," he tells us, "I could not help asking myself over and over again, 'How can this simple . . . powder cost so much money?' for there cannot be gold enough in it, even at that price, to give it this beautiful rich color. It is probably only a better sort of brass; and for brass . . . a dollar and a half an ounce is a marvelous price."

Bessemer hurried home and with a little acid convinced himself that there was no gold in the powder. Here was powdered brass, selling at twenty-two dollars a pound, and the brass itself only cost twenty-two cents a pound.

"This powder must surely be made," he said to himself, "by some old-fashioned hand process, and offers a splendid opportunity for gain, if I can construct a machine to make it."

Bessemer began making a machine that would change, at small cost, a solid block of brass into powder as soft and fine as flour. The first machine he built reduced the solid brass to powder, but when the powder was worked up into paint, it was dull, and lacked the beautiful color that gave value to the powder. "This," he tells us, "was not the first castle I had built, only to see it topple over."

For about a year after this, Bessemer was occupied with other things. But the idea of making a machine that in an hour would give to a pound of brass the value of an ounce of gold haunted him. With the aid of a microscope he studied the bronze powder he had bought, and that which he had made, and saw why his powder was worthless. He then designed and made with his own hands many working models, one to cut the brass, another to roll the tiny particles, another to polish them, and finally one to sift the powder. "At last after months of labor, the great day of trial again arrived. . . . I felt that on the result of this . . . trial hung the whole of my future life's history, and so it did. . . . I watched . . . with a beating heart, and saw the iron monsters do their appointed work."

Bessemer was now sure that he could make bronze powder. He interested in the new enterprise a friend who advanced fifty thousand dollars to build a factory. A patent would give no protection to such an invention. If they were to profit by it, everything must be kept a secret. So Bessemer worked for almost a year in designing all by himself the different machines.

To keep even those who had made the machines from having an idea of what they were for, the different parts of each machine were given out to be made at different places. The old "Baxter House," to become famous because of the many inventions made there in later years, was bought and fitted up for a factory. Here, at length, all the machines were assembled and put in place. To carry on the work — and there was not very much to do, for the machines were all automatic — the three brothers of Bessemer's wife were employed, at extra good wages. They kept faithfully a secret for which at any time they might have received thousands of dollars. The secret did not become known for many years.

BESSEMER AS A YOUNG MAN

The profits from making bronze powder by this new process were enormous. Powder which cost a dollar and thirty cents a pound to make was sold at a dollar and thirty cents an ounce. From these profits, Bessemer had ample means to support himself and his family. In addition, he had sufficient means to carry out and bring to completion the many other inventions born of his active mind. Thus this invention had a profound effect on Bessemer's life. It freed him, at the early age of thirty, from anxiety about the comfort of his family, gave him the use of all of his time, and supplied him with the money necessary to carry on his experiments.

BESSEMER ENJOYS HIS FAMILY

His Master Invention

During the next dozen years, Bessemer was busy with many different projects, and he took out no less than thirty patents. This brings us to 1854, when he was at work on a new kind of ball or projectile for cannon.

PUDDLING MOLTEN METAL

"If you cannot get stronger metal for your guns," said an army officer one day, "such heavy projectiles will be of little use." This remark set Bessemer at work to find a way to produce a metal from which big guns could be cast. This led to the discovery of his now famous process of making steel.

The common way to change pig iron into steel was to break up about seventy pounds of pig iron into small pieces and place them in a tub-like arrangement, over

211

which poured a very hot flame. As the pig iron melted, a man called a puddler stood by and stirred the molten mass so that the flame and air reached all parts of it. After two or three hours of stirring, the liquid iron formed into grains. The heat was then increased until these grains melted and ran together. When this had occurred, the flame was shut off. Then the puddler collected, on the end of an iron bar, the cooling metal in a ball-like mass called a bloom. The bloom was then put between great rollers, and rolled, reheated, and rolled again and again. Or it was hammered, reheated, and hammered over and over. It was this long process, expensive both in fuel and labor, that made steel cost so much.

At the old "Baxter House," Bessemer built a puddling furnace very much like those in common use at that time. One day, when working with his furnace, he noticed two pieces of pig iron on the inside which did not melt, although the heat in the furnace was great. About a half hour later, he observed that the pieces were still unmelted. It occurred to him to take one of them out and examine it. To his surprise, what he thought was a piece of unmelted pig iron turned out to be a piece of steel. He saw from this that if air was forced into the molten pig iron when under great heat, the iron would be changed into steel. A small furnace was built, and Bessemer proved to his own satisfaction that good steel could be produced in this way.

Most people would doubtless have been satisfied with so great a discovery and stopped. But to Bessemer's inquiring mind, this question came: "Yes, pig iron can be changed into steel by forcing air into the molten metal when fuel is used. But can steel be made in this way, without the use of fuel?" The answer to this question changed the history of the world.

Bessemer then built what he called a converter. It was about four feet high, and around the bottom were six pipes extending inside. The pipes were connected on the outside with a chamber into which air was driven by a forced draft.

When all was ready, the draft was turned on, and about seven hundred pounds of molten pig iron were poured into the converter. Except for a few sparks that came from the top, everything went on quietly enough for about ten minutes. Then things began to happen. Clouds of sparks and a roaring flame burst from the top. This was followed by a few mild explosions, and then the converter became a young volcano in active eruption. Slag and white-hot metal were thrown high into the air, and the converter rocked, as explosion followed explosion. All this was a surprise to Bessemer, and for a time he was fearful for his life. In another ten minutes the eruptions had ceased, the flame had died down, and all became quiet again.

The molten metal was hotter than any metal had been heated before. It was drawn off and molded into an ingot. Best of all, it was steel of good quality. Thus was born the most ferocious of all the machines used by men, and one of the greatest of all inventions. "What all this meant," says Bessemer, "what a perfect revolution it threatened in every iron-making district in the world, was fully grasped by my mind as I gazed on that glowing ingot, the mere thought of which almost overwhelmed me for the time."

Bessemer now worked to adapt the new process to commercial use. Many different converters were made, and finally he hit upon the form that has since been in general use. By early August, 1856, he was ready to take out a patent on his invention, which became known the world over as the "Bessemer Process." Thus, in seven months, this great inventor brought forth an invention that changed iron into steel in twenty to thirty minutes, which reduced the cost of making good steel dramatically.

The new invention was scarcely finished before Bessemer read a paper before a meeting of iron makers. The title of his paper, "The Manufacture of Iron (Steel) without Fuel," was the object of many a joke. "We will be burning ice next," remarked one iron maker. "Clay," said another to his friend, "I want you to come with me . . . this morning. Do you know that there is actually a fellow come down from London to read a paper on the manufacture of malleable iron without fuel?" Nevertheless, Bessemer's paper was the sensation of the meeting. Iron makers flocked to "Baxter House" to see the new process. In less than a month, Bessemer sold to

BESSEMER CONVERTER

the iron makers of England licenses to use the new process, to the amount of one hundred and thirty-five thousand dollars. Greater honor and greater wealth than he had ever dreamed of seemed easily within his reach.

Saving the New Process from Failure

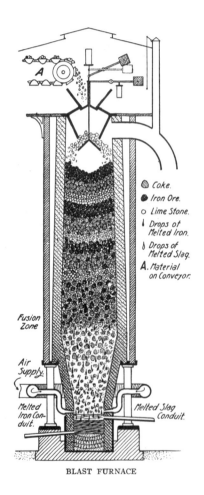

@ Coke.
● Iron Ore.
o Lime Stone.
↓ Drops of Melted Iron.
♭ Drops of Melted Slag.
A. Material on Conveyor.

Fusion Zone

Air Supply.

Melted Iron Conduit.

Melted Slag Conduit.

BLAST FURNACE

Then, lo! The new process proved to be a failure. The steel made by it was good for nothing. The newspapers denounced "the whole scheme as the dream of a wild enthusiast, such as no sensible man could for a moment have entertained." One paper spoke of Bessemer's invention as "a brilliant meteor that had flitted across the . . . sky for a short space, only to die out in a train of sparks, and then vanish into total

216

darkness." These criticisms stunned Bessemer. He went out to the different furnaces and saw for himself the utter failure of his process.

Something was wrong, but he had no idea what it was. Should he give up and admit his failure, or should he go ahead? Bessemer was no "quitter." To protect his family, he gave his wife fifty thousand dollars. This left him sixty thousand, and he resolved to spend the last penny of it, if need be, to prove the worth of his invention.

One expensive experiment followed another, only to end

MAKING PIG IRON

in heartbreaking failure. A whole year, then another half year glided by, with nothing accomplished except that thousands of dollars were spent, and Bessemer was much worn from hard work and anxiety. Those who had something to lose, if his invention was a success, sneered at his efforts. His friends tried to get him to give up a project which experience had shown was worthless. Those dearest to him grieved over his obstinate perseverance. But what could he do? His reputation had been injured; he had spent the greater part of three years and a great fortune on the invention, and he believed in it. To give up was to surrender his reputation, his time, the

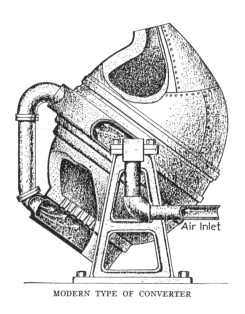

MODERN TYPE OF CONVERTER

money he had invested, and the fame and wealth that he knew would be his if he succeeded. Happily the end was near.

The pig iron produced at this time in England contained considerable phosphorus, and phosphorus was found to be the enemy of the new process. Work as he would, Bessemer could not make good steel out of pig iron with phosphorus in it. He had made good steel, and this led him to wonder what kind of pig iron he had used. He learned that this pig iron came from Sweden, and that it contained no phosphorus. Pig iron from Sweden was immediately ordered. On its arrival, no time was lost in melting it and putting it into the converter. You can well imagine Bessemer's anxiety about the outcome. When the molten mass was turned out of the converter, it was steel of an excellent quality. Not long after this the discovery was also made that with a little care, quantities of pig iron could be produced in England, free from phosphorus. It was now Bessemer's turn to laugh.

Making the Process a Success

Bessemer seemed for a time no nearer to success than before. When he talked to steel makers about buying licenses, they said: "Oh, this is the thing that made such a blaze two years ago, and which was a failure." Not a single steel maker in all England would buy.

Bessemer saw that if his process was ever to be adopted, he must build a steel plant of his own. A plant was started at Sheffield, and Bessemer produced as good steel for fifty dollars a ton as was being sold then for five time this sum. "The only reason," he says, "why the plant was not burned down, was that nobody thought it would come to anything."

When the new steel was made, nobody would buy it. If Bessemer talked to a toolmaker about using some of his metal, he was met with the reply, "Well, perhaps it is good enough for rails. Anything is good enough for rails." On asking a railroad engineer to recommend the use of steel rails, the engineer exclaimed, "Mr. Bessemer, do you wish to see me tried for manslaughter?"

Bessemer's steel was, however, too good, and the price at which it was offered was too attractive to be resisted long by the greedy world. Here and there a toolmaker began to use a little. It was satisfactory, and he bought more. The steel makers, seeing there was a demand for the new metal and that they were being undersold in the market, rushed to Bessemer to obtain licenses to use the new process. Thus began one of the greatest industrial revolutions in modern times. Bessemer's steel gradually found its way into tools, engines, steamboats, cannon, warships, bridges, skyscrapers, and a million other useful things. His royalties from the invention, which even his best friends had at one time considered worthless, amounted to no less than five million dollars.

So many uses were found for steel, after it could be made at little cost, that this era is called the "Age of Steel," and its manufacture became one of the great industries of the world. Great waste regions, like the Mesabi Range of Minnesota, because of the iron ore they contain, became more valuable than gold mines. To transport the enormous quantities of iron ore needed, railroads were built and large ships constructed, which carry nothing else. Large cities like Pittsburgh have grown up around steel, and cities like Gary, Indiana, were located and built for the sole purpose of making it. Billions of dollars are invested in this great industry, and millions of people are employed in it.

Without steel that is both good and inexpensive, we would not have many of our finest and more delicate tools and instruments. We would not have our giant engines, and airplanes, and automobiles. We would not have great bridges, like the Brooklyn Bridge, or our mammoth buildings. Without these and other useful things made of steel, our lives would be very different from what they are, and the whole industrial world about us would be changed.

No wonder Bessemer has been called the "Captain of Modern Civilization," that his discovery is ranked with the printing press and the steam engine as one of the three greatest inventions in the history of the human race, and that his fame is as wide as the world.

STEEL CONSTRUCTION SKYSCRAPERS

Comprehension Questions

1. During what time period did the blast furnace first appear?
2. Where did Henry Bessemer attend high school?
3. What was bronze powder and how was it made?
4. How did Bessemer discover how to make good steel out of pig iron?
5. Why did Bessemer fail to make good steel during his first public trials?

Part III

Inventions of Printing and Communication

Chapter 10

John Gutenberg and the Invention of Printing

When Christopher Columbus was a boy, there were few books. Those he might have read were of two kinds, manuscript books and small block books. Manuscript books were copies of the Bible, or of books of the Greeks and Romans, written out by hand.

PRESS WORK AND TYPESETTING, 1564

223

Persons called copyists made a business of drawing or writing manuscript books. Most of the copyists were monks, who lived in monasteries, where often there was a room set apart for their work, called the writing room. Copying was slow work. To copy a book like the Bible took a year, and when this was done well, it took two or three years.

Manuscript books were written on parchment or vellum.

MONK WRITING ON VELLUM

Parchment is made from the skin of sheep and goats, vellum from the skin of very young lambs and kids. The hair is cut from the skin. The skin is put in a mixture of water and lime, and kept there until the fat is removed. It is then taken out, and stretched and rubbed with pumice stone and lime, until thin and smooth.

The parchment and vellum sheets used in the manuscript books were, as a rule, ten inches wide and fifteen inches long. Broad margins were left on all sides. The first letter of the word beginning the first paragraph on a new page was omitted, as was here and there an important word.

When the copyist had finished his work, the separate sheets were turned over to the illuminator or illustrator. The illustrator filled in the margins with a border of flowers or of foliage, interwoven with birds, animals, angels, or saints. The borders were drawn in blue, green, purple,

ILLUMINATING PAGES OF A MANUSCRIPT BOOK
BY HAND

brown, silver, or gold. The important words omitted were written in color, while elaborate initial letters were painted in at the proper places. These decorations gave to the best manuscript books an elegance and beauty beyond anything to be seen in the common books of today.

Once the illustration was completed, the separate sheets were passed to the bookbinder. Books of large size were bound in boards that were sometimes two inches thick. If the binding was not to be ornamented, the board backs were covered with pigskin. If it was to be ornamented, the covering liked best was calf or goatskin. Upon the ornamentation of the bindings of the best books, there worked gilders, jewelers, engravers, and painters. Some of the most famous books were covered with enameled brass, others with ivory, and still others with gold and silver studded with precious stones.

Because of the work put into them, manuscript books were sold at a high price, and only the rich could afford to buy them. A Bible, only fairly well written and bound, cost from a hundred and fifty to two hundred dollars. At that time the wages of a laborer were fifteen cents a day. The price of a sheep was twenty-five cents; a cow cost two dollars, and a horse cost five dollars.

Block books, on the other hand, were mostly plain, and

PAGE OF THE BIBLE OF THE POOR, A BLOCK BOOK

made up of a few pictures or of illustrations, interspersed with printed explanations or religious precepts. *The Evangelists*, the first of the block books, had, for example, thirty pages. Fifteen of these were printing, while the other fifteen were full-page pictures. The *Bible of the Poor*, the most famous of the block books, consisted of forty pictures. These were seven-and-a-half inches wide, and ten inches long.

The block books were so named, because they were printed from carved or engraved wooden blocks. In making a block book, a piece of oak, ash, cherry, or apple wood was cut two inches think, and the width and length of the desired page. One side of the block, or the face, was smoothed and polished. On this was placed a drawing of the picture, and of the writing to be printed. The surrounding parts of the block were then cut away, to leave the picture and the letters of the writing raised, or in relief, making a sort of stamp. This carving required much skill, and the engraving of a single book consumed weeks and even months.

Once the engraving was completed, the rest was easy. The carved block was covered with a coat of thin ink. A sheet of parchment or paper was placed upon it and pressed gently with the flat back of the inking brush. This transferred an impression of the carved picture and writing to the parchment or paper. The different printed sheets were then bound together.

Any number of books could be printed from the same set of blocks. For this reason block books were cheap. The *ABC's* and the *Lord's Prayer* cost two cents, the *Catechism* twenty cents, *Donatus* or *Boys' Latin Grammar* twelve-and-a-half cents, and the *Bible of the Poor* two dollars. But only small books could be multiplied in this way, for the carving of the blocks was slow work. To prepare the blocks to print the Bible would take at least thirty years, which of course was never done.

Birthplace and Parents of John Gutenberg

John Gutenberg changed all this. He did it by inventing the art of printing from movable type.

Gutenberg was born about the year 1400, at Mainz, a German city on the Rhine, near Frankfort. His parents were of noble blood, and rich landowners, who took a prominent part in the affairs of the city. Nothing is known of Gutenberg's boyhood days, except that they were passed amid scenes of strife between the common people and the nobility.

Learning Two Trades

When John Gutenberg was a boy, it was thought beneath the dignity of one of noble birth to do any ordinary labor, or to learn a trade. Despite this belief, he learned not one, but two trades. He learned the art of cutting and polishing precious stones, and of mirror making.

It is not an easy task today to learn a trade. It was even more difficult when John Gutenberg was a boy. The trades at that time were in the hands of guilds, or, as we would say, trade-unions. Of those in a trade, only the master workmen were allowed to teach it. The number of boys a master workman might take to teach was limited. The boy while learning the trade, which took from five to seven years, received no wages. Instead, he often had to pay a considerable sum for his instruction.

A boy, on undertaking to learn a trade, became an apprentice. As an apprentice, he ran errands, brought tools and materials, took care of the shop, and helped in other ways. After two years or more, he rose to be a journeyman and served another two years. In this period, he learned how to handle and to use tools, and how to do simple kinds of work. In the last two or three years of his service, the journeyman conquered the more difficult parts of the trade. As a kind of final examination he made what was called a masterpiece. This was examined by a committee of master workmen. If they were satisfied with his workmanship, he was admitted to the guild at a great banquet held at his expense, and given the right to set up a business for himself.

A long time to learn a trade? Yes. But John Gutenberg learned two, and at thirty-five was well established at Strassburg with a good paying business. He was also sought out by young men wishing to become cutters of precious stones or makers of mirrors, and was paid for teaching them these arts.

Printing From Movable Type

The idea came to Gutenberg that all words, all writings, all languages are expressed in a small number of different letters. Our language has, for example, only twenty-six letters. With a large number of letters properly set together, a whole page of text could be printed at once. By resetting the different letters, and by repeating the process of printing, large books could be swiftly multiplied. This idea took possession of him, and after 1436, to the neglect of everything else, he gave his time, his energy, and his fortune to working out the process.

The Discovery of Type Metal

Should you go into a newspaper office and see a printing press print, cut, paste, fold, and deliver in sixty minutes forty-eight thousand newspapers of around ninety pages each, it would be natural to think that the most important part of printing is the press. The most important part in printing, however, is the type, or the little movable metal letters. For this reason, the key to inventing printing lay in finding the right kind of metal, and in finding an easy way of making type.

Knowing that block books were printed from carved blocks, Gutenberg first tried to make type from wood. It would seem easy to do this. Yet it proved difficult to carve a good letter upon the end of a small wooden stick. It proved equally hard to cut the sticks of such width that there would be equal spaces between the letters. Even when Gutenberg succeeded in doing this, for he was an expert carver, the ink so softened the wooden type, that after a few impressions, the printed letters became blurred. As the printed letters must be clear and distinct, Gutenberg was forced, much against his will, to give up trying to make movable type from wood.

It now occurred to him that lead would serve. From his work in making mirrors, he knew how easy it was to mold it. With a simple mold he cast a number of small lead sticks of uniform width and height. Then with no great difficulty he carved a letter on the end of each stick. He seemed to be on the direct road to success, but when he came to print from lead type, he found that it took more pressure than with wooden blocks. But when enough

a, MATRIX, AND *b*, PUNCH OF THE LETTER *H*. THE CHARACTERS *D, 1, E*, ARE PRIVATE MARKS OF THE TYPE FOUNDER

pressure was applied to transfer the impression to the paper, it flattened out the lead letters.

Since lead was too soft, Gutenberg thought that iron might do. It proved difficult to mold small iron sticks. The iron stuck to the mold, and the sides of the little sticks were so rough that they would not fit closely together. Expert as Gutenberg was, it was slow work to cut the letters. Worse yet, when the letters were cut, so much pressure had to be used in printing that the hard iron type cut into the paper.

These attempts at making type from wood, lead, and iron took weeks and months. Thus much time and labor seemed lost. Yet this was not all true. For Gutenberg learned from these trials that a metal would have to be found, out of which to make type that could be easily cast. He learned that this metal would have to be harder than lead, but softer than iron. He also learned from trying to cut metal letters, that a mold would have to be invented in which the type could be cast.

As lead could be easily molded, and was then one of the cheapest metals, Gutenberg set about finding a metal to mix with lead, to give it the needed hardness and toughness. Many are the mixtures he must have tried. On one day, this and that combination of lead and copper was tested. On another, lead and brass were combined, now in this and now in that way; and so on, week after week, month after month. Some of the combinations were fairly good, but Gutenberg was never satisfied with half success. He worked on and on, until he hit upon combining five parts of lead, four parts of antimony, and one part of tin. The lead supplied the bulk of the type, the antimony the hardness, and the tin the needed toughness. This mixture of metals proved satisfactory. Strange as it may seem, this type mixture remained about the same until the middle of the twentieth century. No better combination of metal for type has ever been found. It is known as type metal, and is only one of the great discoveries of Gutenberg.

Modern printing presses use a new type of dry or "powdered" ink that is electronically imprinted onto large metal printing sheets known as plates. The images of type or pictures that appear on these plates are then used by the printing press to directly transfer the correct image onto huge rolls of paper that are eventually fashioned into books.

Inventing the Printing Press

No press was needed in making either manuscript or block books. But when Gutenberg tried to print from metal type, he discovered that considerable pressure was required to transfer the likeness of the letters to the parchment or paper. So he had to invent a press that would exert pressure quickly and uniformly.

Gutenberg modeled his printing press after the wine press then in use. It had two upright posts of great strength. These were placed four feet apart, fastened at the bottom to a solid wooden base, and joined at the top by a heavy crossbeam. The middle of this crossbeam held an iron screw worked by a lever. On the lower end of the screw hung a heavy block of wood called the plate, the under side of which was flat and smooth. By turning the screw, the plate could be forced up or down. Between the two upright posts, and upon the base of the press, stood a strong, four-legged stool. This stool served to support a heavy wooden platform, four feet wide and six feet long. Upon this was laid the form, or the wooden frame in which the type was locked. Crude as this printing press was, it served Gutenberg well, and presses like it were the only kind used for more than a hundred and fifty years.

The only ink at the time was the writing fluid of the copyists. Gutenberg found that this was unsatisfactory for printing; instead of forming a thick black coat over the type, it collected in drops and blotted the paper. Another kind of ink had to be made, if printing from metal type was to be a success. The Italian painters had recently invented a new paint composed of lampblack and linseed oil. It was probably from them that Gutenberg got a suggestion that turned him in the right direction. At any rate, he hit upon mixing lampblack and boiled linseed oil, and this mixture proved satisfactory. Printer's ink was made in the same way for hundreds of years.

John Gutenberg's press

Trouble at Strassburg

Gutenberg seemed to be standing upon the threshold of success, but events intervened to rob him of his reward. For several years he had worked night and day on different parts of his invention. Little by little, all the money he had saved, and all he had inherited went into it. To support himself and to continue his work he took three men into partnership. These men paid him a considerable sum of money for their part, and were to share in the profits of the enterprise. As was then the custom, they were sworn to secrecy. Their plan was to complete the invention and print copies of the Bible so common people could enjoy the Word of God. Though Gutenberg and his partners worked steadily for two years, the invention was not complete before the Christmas of 1439.

The cost of the enterprise, the faith of these men, and the will with which they worked are shown in a talk between Andrew Dritzehen, one of the partners, and a Frau von Zabern:

"But will you not stop work, so that you can get some sleep?"

"It is necessary that I first finish this work," said Gutenberg.

"But what a great sum of money you are spending. That has, at least, cost you ten guilders."

"You are a goose; you think this cost but ten guilders. Look here! If you had the money which this has cost, over and above three hundred guilders, you would have enough for all your life. This has cost me at least five hundred guilders. It is but a trifle to what I shall have to spend. It is for this that I have mortgaged my goods and my inheritance."

"But if this does not succeed, what will you do then?"

"It is not possible that we can fail. Before another year is over, we shall have recovered our capital and shall be prosperous."

Dritzehen died a few days later. His death left Gutenberg in a bad plight. The two remaining partners became discouraged and were ready to give up. Frau von Zabern told of her conversation with Dritzehen, and the circumstances of his death caused other people to talk. Gutenberg grew fearful that others would learn of the new art. He sent to Dritzehen's home, and warned the people there to let no one see the press. The molds and type he melted. George, the brother of Andrew, now demanded that he be let into the secret, or that the money Andrew had spent on the enterprise be paid back. Gutenberg refused to tell him of the nature of the undertaking, and claimed that instead of being in debt to Andrew, Dritzehen died in debt to him. The dispute was taken to court, where, after a year of delay, it was settled in favor of Gutenberg.

During the trial, witnesses spoke of the "secret work" Gutenberg was carrying on; they spoke of the "beautiful things," of the "costly things" he was making. No one knew just what he was doing. There was much mystery about the whole enterprise. People began to say: "He doesn't want anyone to know." "He is not willing anyone should see." "Something is wrong." "He is practicing the Black Art."

So great was the prejudice against him, and he was now so poor, that it was impossible for him to go on. He went back to polishing precious stones and making mirrors.

Gutenberg was not long content, however, to work at his trade only. After a year or two, he began to think again of his invention, and to spend his evenings with new type styles and molds. He finally decided to return to Mainz, and set up a printing press.

Printing the First Bible

For four or five years after returning to Mainz, he did what we should call printing jobs. His success was so noticeable that a rich money lender became interested. Their plan was to print the complete Bible. It was to be printed in Latin, and was to look in every way like the best of the manuscript books.

The pages were printed in two columns of forty-two lines each. These columns, with the space between of five

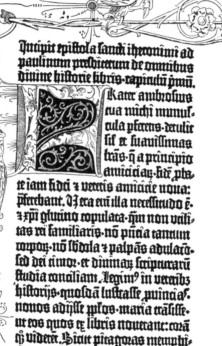

PART OF A PAGE OF GUTENBERG'S BIBLE

eighths of an inch, made a page eleven-and-a-half inches long and seven-and-three-fourths inches wide. Large spaces were left for initial letters, and a wide margin was allowed for a border. It often happened that the space for the initial letter and for the border was not filled in. Yet some early printed books rival in beauty of decoration the most famous manuscript books.

The entire Bible, when printed in this way, covered twelve hundred and eighty-two pages, and was bound in two large volumes. It is known as Gutenberg's first Bible, and was the first great work to come from the printing press. An undecorated copy on paper could be had then for four dollars. A decorated copy on vellum was recently sold in London for over one hundred thousand dollars.

Cheated by Fust

When Gutenberg entered upon the bold plan of printing the entire Bible, he thought he could have it ready for sale within three years. Plan and toil as he might, three years passed, four years went by, and it was late in the fifth, or toward the end of 1455, before the printed pages were ready to be bound. Yet at last, after five years of disappointment, hard work, and trials, the task was done, and the printed Bible was ready for sale.

PRINTING BOOKS IN 1520

But Fust, the money lender, did not go into partnership with Gutenberg to help him perfect a great invention, and to aid him in printing the greatest of all books. He thought that he saw in the new art a means of making money. He had invested a large sum in the enterprise. After five years, not one cent of this had been returned, nor had he received one penny of profit. This was too much for the money-greedy Fust. With the Bible printed and ready for sale, he saw his opportunity. He would seize the molds, the type, the presses, and all the printed Bibles. In this way he could get back all, and even more than he had invested. To do this, he brought suit in the court for the return of all the money he had spent on the undertaking. An unjust judge decided in his favor. As Gutenberg had no way of paying such a large sum, Fust seized everything, and turned Gutenberg out.

Gutenberg was not, however, to be neglected in his old age. As a reward for his services to the church and to the world, the Archbishop of Mainz made him, in 1465, a gentleman at court, and gave him a pension for life. The pension supplied him with a home, food, and clothing, for the quaint document reads: "We will clothe him every year, always like our noblemen, and give him our court dress."

Gutenberg was not to enjoy his leisure or the honors of a nobleman long. In February 1468, he became sick and died. He was laid to rest at Mainz, Germany.

Honor Paid Gutenberg

Though he died loaded down with debts, and with but few friends by his side, great honors were to come to him as the inventor of the greatest of the modern arts. On one of the first tablets erected to his memory is this inscription: "To John Gutenberg, of Mainz, who, first of all, invented molding letters in brass, and by this art has deserved honor from the whole world." Monuments honoring him are now to be found in many places. His greatest monument will survive them all. It is the printed book in the hands of common people.

ILLUMINATED LETTER.

Comprehension Questions

1. What was the name given to people who used to write manuscripts by hand?
2. Where was John Gutenberg born?
3. Why did the invention of the printing press lower the cost of books?
4. What was the name of the first book that Gutenberg printed on his press?
5. How did Mr. Fust cheat Gutenberg?

John Gutenberg was the inventor of a new way of printing.

He printed the whole line at once in a book instead of making one letter at a time, as had to be done in block printing. After he was through with this line, he threw all the little letters back into the boxes again, so that he could use some of the same letters over for the next line. A little later he had enough letters so that he could print a whole page at once. Of course he could then print much more quickly.

Chapter 11

Samuel F. B. Morse
and the Invention of the Telegraph

Sending messages is an older form of communication than writing or printing. The American Indians, for example, used a system of signal fires at night to send messages telling of victories or of danger. In the daytime they held blankets over a fire, so as to signal by means of columns of smoke. Messages were sent also by sound signals made either by mouth or by drum. As time went on, a system of signaling by flags and lanterns was developed by the United States Army and the Navy. This manner of sending messages was used during the 1700s and early 1800s.

The Signal Telegraph

The first practical message system similar to telegraphing, was invented in 1794 by the three Chappe brothers, while they were only boys attending boarding school. The rules were strict, and did not allow them to visit each other as often as they wanted to. They could see each other from the windows of their rooms so they worked out a way of sending messages. A board with a small crossbeam at each end was hung on a pivot. The board and crossbeams could be moved by cords, like the arms of a jumping puppet. Each position of the beam and a crossbeam stood for a letter. With this device, it was easy for these boys to spell out messages to each other.

The French government bought the device from the Chappe brothers, building signal stations along the coast, and between Paris and the more important cities. In 1840 there were 1400 miles of signal telegraph. The stations were about three miles apart. The crossbeams of the signal towers were furnished with lights, so that messages could be sent by night as well as by day. An operator could spell out a hundred words an hour.

SIGNAL TELEGRAPH OF 1840

A system of signaling like that invented by the Chappe brothers was introduced into Russia and England also. There was a line, for example, seventy miles long between London and Portsmouth.

An Englishman wrote in 1828 that the telegraph carried information speedily and distinctly, and that it could be constructed and maintained at little expense.

A similar system was used in America, only large letters were used instead of crossbeams, to spell out the words.

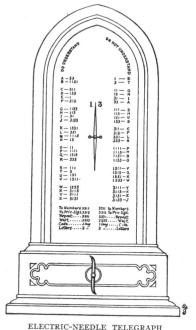

ELECTRIC-NEEDLE TELEGRAPH

Lines were maintained, for example, between New York and Sandy Hook, and between New York and Philadelphia.

The Electric Telegraph

"Take this message as quick as lightning," was doubtless an expression often used in connection with messages. It was not a far step from thinking of taking a message as "quick as lightning," to thinking of making lightning carry the message. Messages were sent by electric telegraph as early as 1774. Every few years after that, some inventor brought forward a new system. Hundreds of men were busy, and in 1838 there were upwards of sixty different systems in the field, each inventor working hard to make his the best.

Steinheil's Electric Telegraph

Oersted learned in 1819, that to make the needle of a compass turn to the left or to the right, all that is necessary is to hold a wire near the compass, parallel with the needle, and send an electric current over the wire toward the north or toward the south. Less than a month afterwards, a French scientist pointed out how this discovery could be used in telegraphing messages.

In 1833, Gauss and Weber, two noted German scientists, put up an electric-needle telegraph line, about a mile long. Wires were stretched around a permanent magnet hung at the center on a silk thread. By changing the direction of the electric current, the magnet was turned, at will, to the right or to the left. One turn of the magnet to the right stood for the letter *a*. One turn to the left stood for *e*. Two turns to the right stood for *i*, and so on. Here is the complete telegraphic alphabet of Gauss and Weber. It has often been used by boys and girls, to signal messages to each other, with their hands and arms.

```
r    = a        rrr  = ck       lrl  = m
lrrr = w        llrr = 4        l    = e
rrl  = d        rll  = n        rrll = z
lllr = 5        rr   = i        rlr  = f  v
rrrr = p        rlrl = o        llrl = 6
rl   = o        lrr  = g        rrrl = r
rllr = 1        lrll = 7        lr   = u
lll  = h        rrlr = s        lrrl = 2
rlll = 8        ll   = b        llr  = I
rlrr = t        lrlr = 3        llll = 9
```

With this code Gauss and Weber sent all kinds of messages. Being too busy to work on their telegraph, they turned it over to Steinheil. Steinheil built and put into use, at Munich in 1837, his Registering Electro-Magnetic Telegraph. The line was five miles long. Two permanent magnets were hung in the center of a coil of wire. Each magnet could be made, at will, to swing out from the coil. On an arm fastened to the end of each magnet was a little cup for ink. At the bottom and side of the cup was a printing needle. When the magnet swung out, the printing needle touched a moving ribbon of paper, and printed a dot. Dot signals were thus recorded on the paper in two lines.

Steinheil could send messages at the rate of six words a minute, or three hundred and sixty words an hour. His system was adopted by the Bavarian government, and was in use for many years.

Wheatstone and Cook's Electric Telegraph

Charles Wheatstone, of London, and his business partner also patented, in 1837, an electric-needle telegraph. Five needles were fastened in the center of a diamond-shaped dial, on which the alphabet and numerals were printed. To signal a letter, one needle was turned to the right, and one to the left. The letter signaled was the one at the point where lines running down from the points of the needle crossed. To signal a number, only one needle was turned. A line twenty miles long was built, in 1838, on the Great Western Railway. To send messages, it took six wires, one wire to turn each of the five needles, and one to complete the electric circuit, making the system expensive. So, Wheatstone invented a two-needle system, and later a single-needle system. From 1838 on, Wheatstone's electric-needle telegraph was in constant use, and for years was the only system that found favor in England.

Morse's Electric Telegraph

Many of the great scientists of Europe thus worked to invent a successful system of electric telegraph. But it remained for an American, Samuel F. B. Morse, to invent the most successful system. Morse's system of electric telegraph was so simple, and messages could be sent by it so quickly, that it drove almost every other system out of business. For this reason, Morse is called the inventor of the electric telegraph, although strictly speaking, that title does not belong to him. He is, however, the inventor of the most successful system; and for his great service in giving to the world this useful invention, he is worthy of the highest honor. The Morse telegraph system was the main communication system in the world for almost a century.

Morse's Education

Samuel Finley Breese Morse was born in 1791, at Charlestown, Massachusetts. He was given the best education that was to be had at the time. When seven years old he was sent away from home to a famous private school, Phillips Academy. There he prepared for Yale College (now Yale University), entering with the class of 1807, and completing the course in 1810.

In those days the sciences did not receive much attention at college. In the little that was taught, Morse took an unusual interest. He studied both chemistry and physics, and he learned almost all there was to be known then about electricity and electric batteries. Once Professor Day, his teacher in physics, sent a current of electricity through a chain in a dark room. Flashes of light could be seen between the links. How little Professor Day knew at the time of the influence this experiment was to have! Many years afterwards, Morse said: "The fact that . . . electricity can be made visible at any . . . part of a circuit was the crude seed which took root in my mind, and grew . . . and finally ripened into the invention of the telegraph."

Morse the Artist

Morse, like Fulton, started out to be an artist. At college, he painted miniatures for a number of his classmates. Though he had had no lessons in either drawing or painting, his classmates liked their pictures and paid him a good price for them.

After his graduation from college, Morse decided to study art. Like Fulton, he went to London to work with Benjamin West, where he remained for four years, not returning home until 1815.

He was then twenty-four years old, and up to that time had been supported by his father. He now opened a studio in Boston. Hundreds of people came to see his "Judgment of Jupiter," one of the pictures he had painted in London and which had attracted much attention there. All who came admired it, but none offered to buy it or order a picture. After waiting a year without receiving a single order, he returned to painting miniatures.

As a wandering artist in Vermont and New Hampshire, he

MORSE PAINTING THE PORTRAIT OF LAFAYETTE. THIS PORTRAIT IS. NOW IN CITY HALL, NEW YORK

did well. He was even more successful at Charleston, South Carolina, where he went in the winter of 1818. There he had requests for all the portraits he could paint. In a single week one hundred and fifty were ordered, at sixty dollars apiece. He was so successful that in the fall of the first year, he returned to New England, taking his bride back to Charlestown with him. There they lived for three years, saving in that time several thousand dollars. But Morse was not content to remain a portrait painter. He decided to leave Charlestown, and take up what he felt was his true work, the painting of historical pictures. So he moved his family to New Haven, Connecticut.

For eighteen months, he worked early and late on a picture of the House of Representatives. The picture was eleven feet long and seven and a half feet high, with the Representatives on one side, and the Senators on the other. In all, it contained eighty portraits. The picture when finished was exhibited at Boston, but few people took the trouble to see it. No one wanted to buy it, and the whole venture turned out a failure.

Morse soon afterwards travelled to New York, and again began to paint portraits. His progress at first was slow. "My cash is almost gone," he wrote to his wife. "I have advertised, and visited, and hinted, and pleaded, and even asked one man to sit, but all to no avail."

Morse was so discouraged that he even thought of going to Mexico City. But better days were at hand. General Lafayette was visiting this country, and New York gave Morse an order for a life-size portrait of the Frenchman. For this he received a thousand dollars.

In the midst of his blessings, Morse was called upon to bear the loss of his wife. Though heartbroken, he went on with his work. He soon had all the portraits he could paint, and came in time to be looked upon as the greatest artist in America. He not only painted portraits, but he gave talks on art, and was the leader in organizing the National Academy of the Arts.

Still, Morse was not satisfied with his success. To prepare himself to paint the great pictures of which he dreamed — pictures which he believed would bring fame to him and honor to his country — he decided to spend three more years in Europe. During these three years, he visited great art galleries and studied the paintings of the great masters.

Planning the Electric Telegraph

In October 1832, Morse sailed for home on the oceanliner *Sully*. There was considerable talk among the passengers

about electricity. The discoveries of Oersted, Faraday, and Sturgeon were attracting wide attention. Morse was led one day to say: "I see no reason why intelligence may not be sent by electricity." This was a new thought to him. So far as he then knew, no one had ever before thought of sending messages by electricity. The new idea filled his mind. It not only haunted him in the daytime, but it kept him from sleep at night. On leaving the boat he said, "Well, captain, should you hear of the telegraph one of these days, as the wonder of the world, remember that the discovery was made on board the good ship *Sully*."

Making the First Instrument

Morse was scarcely off the ship, before he was telling his brothers about his new idea. Instead of telling his artist friends about what he saw in the great art galleries of Europe, and about the pictures he had painted, he talked to them, to their disgust, about his electric telegraph. Many people wanted Morse to paint portraits for them, for he was easily the best prepared and the most successful artist in America. But he wanted all the time he could get to work on his invention, and therefore he painted only enough to earn a scanty living. But work as he would, five years passed by before he was even able to complete a working model.

During most of these years he lived in a single room, which served alike for studio, parlor, bedroom, kitchen, and workshop. "In order to save time to carry out my invention," said Morse afterwards, "and to save my limited funds, I had for many months lodged and eaten in my studio, getting my food in small quantities from some grocery, and preparing it myself. To conceal from my friends the poverty in which I lived, I was in the habit of bringing my food to my room in the evenings, and this

FIRST MORSE INSTRUMENT AND KEY

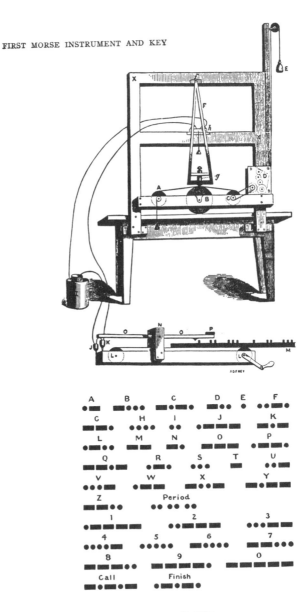

THE MORSE CODE

was my mode of life for many years."

Morse was not ready to show his electric telegraph to the public until September 1837. His telegraphic code was simple. One dot "." stood for "1". Two dots ". ." stood

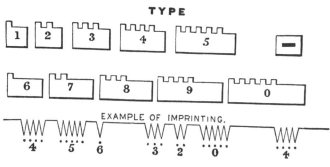

SAMPLES OF TYPE AND OF WRITING WITH AN IMPROVED TELEGRAPH INSTRUMENT

for "2". One dot "." and a dash "-" stood for "6", and so on for each of the numerals and zero. For each number of the telegraphic code, there was a metal type. There was also a telegraphic dictionary in which given numbers stood for given words. For example, 215 stood for successful.

Morse's first instrument was very crude, and the method of sending and recording messages was slow and clumsy.

But to those who for the first time saw messages sent by electric telegraph, the invention seemed wonderful. Besides, Morse had thought of something of which none of the great scientists of Europe had dreamed. In Steinheil's electric telegraph, the signals were recorded by the movement of a magnetic needle. Wheatstone also made use of the magnetic needle. But Morse employed the electromagnet of Sturgeon and of Henry to record the signals in his system, and it was this use of the electromagnet that made the Morse system the most successful of all.

Improving the Invention

Up to the time Morse showed his invention to the public in 1837, no one had helped him on it. Being anxious to perfect it, and if possible to get money from Congress to carry out an experiment on a large scale, he now took into partnership Professor Gale, of New York University, who was to work on the electric batteries; and also Alfred Vail, who was to furnish the money needed and help with the instruments.

During the fall of 1838, the clumsy telegraphic dictionary and code numbers on which Morse had spent many a day was done away with, and a system of dots and dashes for each of the letters of the alphabet and different numbers was planned. This telegraphic code is like the codes of Gauss and Weber, and of Steinheil. It is known the world over as the Morse code.

The clumsy way of recording the telegraphic signal by dashes and V-shaped figures was also done away with. The recording instrument was modified, so that it now wrote the dots and dashes which stood for the letters and numbers. In the meantime Professor Gale had so improved the batteries that an electric current could be sent through ten miles of copper wire.

Morse exhibited the improved instrument to his New York friends in January 1838. "Seeing is believing," but what they saw, they could at first scarcely believe. Message after message, at the rate of ten words a minute, was sent over the ten miles of wire, until the admiration of the company was unbounded. They cheered the inventor and congratulated him on his great invention. Morse received this letter from his brother Sidney: "Your invention, measuring it by the power it will give man to carry out his plans, is not only the greatest invention of this age, but the greatest invention of any age. I see . . . that the surface of the earth will be networked with wire, and every wire will be a nerve, carrying to every part intelligence of what is happening in every other part. . . . No limit can be set to the value of the invention!"

Seeking Aid

Morse now took his invention to Washington, D.C., and asked Congress to give him thirty thousand dollars to build a telegraph line between Washington and Baltimore. This seemed a large sum of money to spend on an untried enterprise. It was also hard for men to understand how useful the telegraph would be. Congress refused to vote the money.

Morse knew that both England and France were spending large sums on their signal-telegraph systems. If they could only see his invention, they would adopt it at once. But he had no money for a trip to Europe. To get it, he took a third partner. The invention was exhibited in London and Paris. Statesmen and scientists came to see it, and Morse was declared a great genius, and was highly honored. Indeed, at one time it seemed as if both France and Russia would adopt his system, but in the end nothing was done. Returning to America in the spring of 1839, he wrote: "I return without a penny in my pocket, and have to borrow even for my meals."

The next four years were the darkest in Morse's life. His partners had spent all their money, and at times lost interest. Congress continued to refuse to vote the thirty thousand dollars. Morse had neglected his art so long that it was hard for him to get pupils to teach, or portraits to paint. Many a morning when he rose, he scarcely knew where the food for the day was to come from.

Once, when a pupil was late in paying for his lessons, he nearly starved.

"Well, my boy," asked Morse, "how are you set for money?"

"Why, professor," replied the student, "I am very sorry to say I have been disappointed; but I expect money next week."

"Next week, I shall be dead by that time."

A MODERN TELEGRAPH

"Dead, sir?"

"Yes, dead of starvation."

265

"Would ten dollars be of any service?"

"Ten dollars would save my life; that is all it would do."

The student paid the money, and the two dined together. After the meal was over Morse said, "This is my first meal in twenty-four hours."

These years of delay, though hard to bear, were not lost. With the help of Professor Gale and the advice of Professor Henry, of Princeton, the batteries were improved. So when Congress at last voted the money for the line between Washington and Baltimore, an electric current could be sent through the wires for the entire forty miles. With the help of Mr. Vail, the metal types and the clumsy machine for sending the signals were done away with. A simple finger key was invented to send the dots and dashes. When the metal types were used, only ten words a minute could be sent. With the finger key, an operator could easily send twenty to thirty words a minute. Without these improvements, Morse's electric telegraph would have been a failure when put to the test in 1844.

Morse was tempted quite often to give up. But the thought that his invention marked a new era in history, and would improve the condition of millions of people, kept him from it. In the winter of 1843, he went once more to Washington, seeking the aid of Congress. Columbus himself was scarcely more persevering under discouragement. On the day his bill passed the House of Representatives, Morse wrote to Mr. Vail: "For two years I have labored all my time, and at my own expense, without assistance from the other proprietors, to forward our enterprise. My ability to pay my expenses is nearly all gone. If the bill should fail in the Senate, I shall return to New York with the fraction of a dollar in my pocket." "Had the passage of the bill failed," he wrote to a friend, "there would have been little prospect of another attempt on my part to introduce to the world my new invention."

The Bill Passed

On the evening of the last day of the session, Morse sat waiting in the gallery of the Senate. He was told by friendly Senators that there was no chance for his bill to pass, so he finally went to his room. "Knowing from experience that my help must come from God in any difficulty," wrote Morse, "I soon disposed of my cares, and slept as quietly as a child."

On coming down to breakfast the next morning, he was met by the daughter of a friend.

"Why this early call?" asked Morse.

"I have come to congratulate you."

"Indeed, for what?"

"On the passage of your bill."

"Oh, no, my young friend, you are mistaken."

TELLING MORSE ABOUT THE PASSAGE OF THE BILL

"It is you that are mistaken. The bill was passed at midnight."

The news was so unexpected that Morse for the moment could not speak. Finally he said, "You are the first to tell me, and the first message on the completed line between Washington and Baltimore shall be yours."

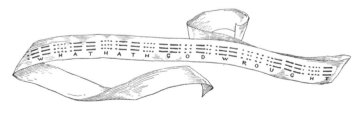

Samuel F. B. Morse

The First Telegraph Line

In constructing the new line, Morse planned to put the telegraph wires in a lead pipe and then bury the pipe in the ground. After ten miles of lead pipe had been laid, it was discovered that the electric current would not pass through a single mile of it. Twenty thousand of the thirty thousand dollars voted by Congress had been spent. What was to be done? It was decided to place the wires on poles with short crossarms just as you see telephone wires today. Thinking it was necessary to insulate them, the wires were wrapped in cotton cloth soaked in tar and beeswax, and fastened on door knobs to the crossarms. From now on, the work progressed rapidly. The whole line was finished and opened in May 1844. Morse remembered his promise, and the young lady selected these noble words: "What hath God wrought!" Of this message Morse said, "It baptized the American telegraph with the name of its Author." To God be the glory, great things He has done!

Receiving the Reward

It was a favorite idea with Morse that the government should own the telegraph. After it was shown to be a success, he offered to sell it for one hundred thousand dollars. Fortunately for Morse, the government refused the offer, for few inventions have been more quickly and widely adopted. A line was completed in 1846 between Baltimore and New York. Within the next ten years, telegraph companies sprang up in every section of our country. Most of these combined, and formed a single company, called Western Union in 1857. His system was adopted in Canada, then in Europe, and before he died in 1872, was used in every civilized country of the world. Morse lived, therefore, to see the whole world bound together by the telegraph; each part able to know what was going on in every other part; each part able to communicate and to do business with every other part. Thus, by means of the electric telegraph, the countries of the world were able to communicate with each other for the first time with great speed.

Comprehension Questions

1. Who invented the "Registering Electro-Magnetic Telegraph?"
2. Where was Samuel Morse born?
3. What special skill did Mr. Morse have before he became an inventor?
4. How did the invention of the telegraph help to revolutionize world communication?
5. What was the first message sent over the Morse telegraph line in May 1844?

Chapter 12

Alexander Graham Bell
and the Invention of the Telephone

The electric telegraph of Morse was a wonderful invention. A still more wonderful method of sending messages was to be found. There is scarcely a boy or girl old enough to read this book, who has not used the telephone time and time again. So useful is the telephone, that it would now be very difficult for the world to get along without it. Yet it was not invented until 1876. The inventor was Alexander Graham Bell.

Birthplace and Education

Alexander Graham Bell was born at Edinburgh, Scotland, in 1847. He was educated at the Royal High School of Edinburgh, and also attended the University of Edinburgh and the University of London. From boyhood, he was taught at home by his father, about sound and oral speech, and he also received training in music. When he was more than sixty years old, he wrote the following account of his early experiences.

"As I look back and see what points in my early life had an influence on this result, I think that one important element was my love of music. I could play the piano before I could read or write. I could play anything by ear. . . . . In fact as a little chap I was considered quite a musical prodigy, by a distinguished Italian teacher . . . who, when I was about nine or ten years of age, took me under his charge to make a musician of me, but he did not succeed. Anyway, I had this love of music. I could play all sorts of musical instruments in a sort of a way. . . . . I also knew how the different musical instruments were made. I was just as familiar with beating reeds and free reeds, and the way in which the sounds were produced, as a person could be who had really studied the subject.

"A second element was of even greater importance. I came from a family that had made a . . . study of oral speech for two generations before me. My grandfather, Alexander Bell, a distinguished teacher of speech in London, was the first. Both of his sons — my father, Alexander Melville Bell, and my uncle, David Charles Bell — took up the same work. They also . . . devoted their attention to the correction of defects of speech. People who lisped, or stammered, or did any thing of that sort, came to my father, to be taught, for example, how to place the organs of speech in forming sounds.

"In my early boyish days, I had the destructive faculty very fully developed. My toys never remained whole in my hands. I would always pull them to pieces to see how they were made, and one of my earliest studies in that respect was plants. I had a delight in pulling plants to pieces to see how they were made. When I was quite a little fellow, I actually took up the study of botany, and I had my collection of plants. My father encouraged me in it. He always encouraged me in making collections of all sorts, and that is a most important thing in the case of a boy. He taught me to observe, compare, and classify. I passed through the stamp-collecting age, the egg age, and the coin age, but the things I took most interest in were the flowers.

"There was another thing which now, as I look back upon it, was of the greatest consequence in its bearing upon the telephone. My father encouraged his boys to study everything relating to the mechanism of speech. We were very much interested in reading of the construction of an automation speaking machine . . .

"My father proposed to his boys that they should try to make a speaking machine. . . . The work was parceled out between my brother Melville and myself. He was to make the lungs and the throat, and the vocal chords, and I was to undertake the mouth. . . . I made a mouth modeled . . . from a skull. . . . My brother had finished his larynx about the same time that I had made the mouth, and it was a great day when we put the two together. We did not wait for the wind chest that was to represent the lungs . . . but we stuck the thing together. My brother blew through the tube that was to lead from the wind chest, and I took the lips of my machine and moved them. Out came a sound like a Punch and Judy show, and we were delighted when we moved the lips up and down to hear 'Ma-ma! Ma-ma!' distinctly . . .

TESTING THEIR TALKING MACHINE ON THE NEIGHBORS

"My father used the machine to impress upon us the mechanism of speech, but we cared more for the effects produced. I remember very well, one time, when my brother and I took this machine out to the common stairway at Edinburgh. . . . My brother blew, and there came a sound like a regular squalling baby, 'Ma-ma! Ma-ma!' in a most distressing tone of voice. Then we were perfectly delighted to hear a door open upstairs and some person come out. When we made it cry for all it was worth, we heard someone say, 'My goodness! What is the matter with the baby?' That was just what we wanted. We crept into our own house softly and shut the door and left our neighbors to look for the baby.

"There came another period in which I took up what might be termed scientific research. . . . Now a controversy arose . . . between my father and myself . . . He had shown that when you whisper vowel sounds you hear musical effects; and when you whisper the vowels in the order in which he had them in his system of Visible Speech, he would . . . hear an ascending scale of musical tones, whereas I as distinctly heard a descending scale . . . To my ear 'E' gave the highest sound and 'Ah' the lowest; to my father's ear 'E' gave the lowest sound and 'Ah' gave the highest. We really had a heated argument over it, until I made the discovery . . . that there were two series of musical tones, one going down and the other going up. My father was convinced that we were both right . . . He advised me — I was only sixteen then — to communicate my discovery to a most distinguished man on the subject of phonetics and sound in Great Britain, Alexander Ellis.

"I wrote to him and sent him my analysis of sounds. . . . I received a note from Mr. Ellis telling me that I had made a great discovery, but that someone had made it before me. The man who did it was a man by the name of Helmholtz, a great German physicist.

"I went to see Mr. Ellis, and he showed me Helmholtz's book. It was in German and I could not read German, but Mr. Ellis tried to tell me about Helmholtz. He said . . . Helmholtz had not only analyzed vowel sounds, but had reproduced them by tuning forks . . . set in vibration by an electric current, . . . and I knew nothing of electricity. How I wished I knew how those tuning forks were set in vibration!

"In my ignorance of electricity, I had a curious delusion, and that again had something to do with the telephone. I had the idea, in my ignorance of what Helmholtz had really done, that he had transmitted vowel sounds by electricity; that he had reproduced at the other end of a telegraph line, with those tuning forks, the various vowel sounds. That was my idea. It was all wrong. He never had any such idea, he never did any such thing, but that was my idea, and it occurred to me: 'If Helmholtz could transmit and reproduce vowel sounds, you could reproduce consonant sounds as well; you could reproduce speech.'

"About this time my two brothers died of a strange disease. As I had overtaxed my own health by working too hard — I was teaching by day and studying by night - my father insisted on my stopping all work and going with him to Canada. He bought a farm near Brantford, Ontario, and for some months I lived out of doors."

Teacher of the Deaf and Dumb

"My father had suggested a use of his system of pictorial symbols representing the position of the vocal organ in forming sounds . . . which caught my fancy . . . . He said: 'Here are symbols which have again and again enabled people to pronounce . . . Why, then, might it not be possible through this means to teach the deaf and dumb, who have never heard English, to use their mouths?' I became infatuated with this idea and formed a plan for teaching the deaf and dumb." It was not long before Bell had an opportunity to put his idea into practice. The

Board of Education of Boston employed him to teach in the public school for the deaf, and he began his work in April 1871.

"The teachers in the school for the deaf had been trying to teach the children to speak, and had met with good success. But the teachers made a claim that seemed to me to be ridiculous. They claimed not only that deaf children could be taught to speak . . . but that after they had been taught to speak, they could come to understand speech by looking at the mouth of the speaker . . . I did not dare to say no, but I did not believe it, and out of my skepticism about lip reading grew the telephone."

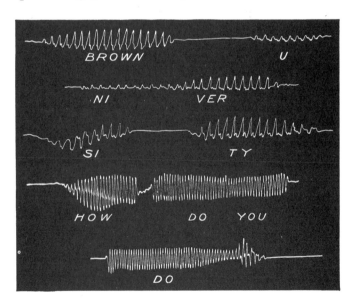

SOUND WAVES MADE WITH HUMAN EAR APPARATUS

Bell worked to develop a series of sound pictures, so that deaf children might learn to speak by sight. One of the instruments with which he worked was the phonautograph. The phonautograph used by Bell was a large cone, closed at the small end by a membrane of goldbeater's skin. Hung at one edge of the membrane and attached to the center was a light wooden lever. The

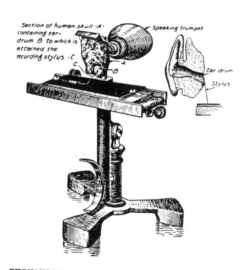

PHONAUTOGRAPH TRACINGS ON SMOKED GLASS

other end of the lever extended forward beyond the membrane, and on the end of it was fastened a pig's bristle. Speak into the phonautograph, and the membrane and lever will vibrate, or move back and forth. The vibration of the bristle at the end of the lever traces a zigzag line on a smoked glass drawn underneath. Each sound, "A", "E", etc., has its own vibration or sound picture. Bell's idea was to photograph these sound pictures; then give the deaf child the sound picture of, for example, "A," and put him to work to produce on the phonautograph a sound that would make a similar zigzag line. In this way the child would learn to sound the different letters.

"It struck me," says Bell, "that in the phonautograph, there was a remarkable resemblance to the human ear.

"I went to a distinguished aurist of Boston, and told him I wanted to make a phonautograph, modeling it after the ear. He replied, 'Why don't you use a human ear itself, taken from a dead man, as a phonautograph?' That was quite a new idea, and I said, 'I shall be very glad to do that, but where can I get a dead man's ear?' 'Oh,' he said, 'I will get it for you,' and he did. This was in 1874.

"When my summer vacation came, I ran up to Brantford, Ontario, to spend the time with my parents. I took the human ear with me in order to get tracings. I moistened the membrane with glycerine and water, attached a piece of hay to one of the little bones, and rigged up an apparatus for dragging a piece of smoked glass underneath. Through a speaking trumpet I spoke into that dead man's ear, and obtained beautiful tracings of the vibrations upon smoked glass."

Birth of the Telephone

From his study of Helmholtz, Bell thought he saw how to use tuning forks, vibrated by an electric current, to send at one time many telegraph messages over one wire. Bell called his invention the multiple or harmonic telegraph. But up to the time he left Brantford for Boston, in April 1871, the multiple telegraph was merely an idea.

TALKING IN FIRST FORM OF TELEPHONE

After reaching Boston, Bell was busy instructing teachers how to teach deaf children to talk, and in teaching little deaf children himself. There were many deaf children whose parents were willing to pay almost any sum to have them taught to speak, and Bell was so successful in doing this that he opened a private school of his own in October 1872. To this school there came deaf-mutes, teachers of the deaf and dumb, and persons with defective speech. Bell also took complete charge of the education of a deaf child, George Sanders, and often gave public talks to interest people in the education of the deaf.

In the fall of the next year, Bell went to Salem, Massachusetts, to make his home with the grandmother of his little pupil, George Sanders. In the attic of his new home he fixed up a workroom. This was supplied with tuning forks, reeds, magnets, electric batteries, wire, and the like. His days were spent in Boston at his school, but many an evening found him in his attic workshop, busy with his multiple telegraph.

"Often in the middle of the night Bell would wake me up," said Thomas Sanders, the father of George. "His black eyes would be blazing with excitement. Leaving me to go up to the attic, he would rush wildly to the barn and begin to send me signals along his experimental line. If I noticed any improvement in his machine, he would be delighted. He would leap and whirl around in one of his 'war dances,' and then go contentedly to bed. But if the experiment was a failure, he would go back to his bench and try some different plan."

When Bell arrived at Brantford, in the summer of 1874, he was thus carrying on two studies. He was working on his multiple telegraph, and he was trying to make tracings of the vibrations of sounds so as to get sound pictures to use in teaching the deaf.

Bell had with him, as has been said, a phonautograph made from a dead man's ear. "As I was holding the human ear in my hand, it struck me," says Bell, "that the bones of that human ear were very massive compared to the membrane. The membrane was like a little piece of tissue paper, hardly the size of a finger nail, and the bones that were moved by the little membrane were really very heavy. It suddenly occurred to me, that if such a small membrane as that would move bones so massive in comparison, why would not a larger membrane move my piece of iron? At once the idea of a membrane speaking telephone became complete in my mind. All I had to do was to attach a steel reed, not tuned to any definite pitch, to the center of a stretched membrane, just as in the phonautograph, so that it would vibrate in front of an electromagnet, and put another at the end of a telegraph wire, and we would have . . . a speaking telephone."

The idea of a membrane electric-speaking telephone was thus complete in Bell's mind in the summer of 1874. But he did not try to make one, for he felt it would not work. On his return to Boston, in the fall of 1874, Bell succeeded in interesting Thomas Sanders and Gardner Hubbard in his ideas. Sanders was the father of George Sanders, the little boy who was being instructed by Bell, and Hubbard was the father of Mabel Hubbard, also one of his pupils. Sanders and Hubbard promised to pay the cost of Bell's experiments. But he gave his time chiefly to the multiple telegraph, because they thought this invention would be more profitable than the telephone.

The next year was full of work. Bell toiled day and night, making experiment after experiment. Such was the progress on the multiple telegraph, that an application for a patent was made in February 1875, for "Improvement in Transmitting Telegraph Messages." The patent was granted in April 1875. Like so many other patents, nothing ever came of the multiple telegraph, though Bell worked on it for some years to come.

Making the First Telephone

Bell's hard but fruitless work on the multiple telegraph weakened his courage. At one time he was about ready to give up trying to invent a telephone, but was

encouraged to go on by the same great man who helped
Morse, Professor Henry. Bell visited Henry, to consult
with him about some experiments connected with the
multiple telegraph. "I felt so much encouraged by his
interest," wrote Bell to his parents, "that I decided to ask
his advice about the apparatus I have designed for the

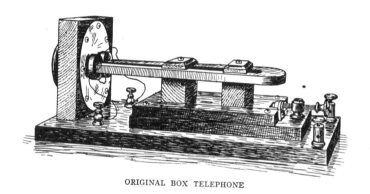

ORIGINAL BOX TELEPHONE

transmission of the human voice. I explained the idea and
said: 'What would you advise me to do, publish it and let
others work it out, or attempt to solve the problem
myself?' He said he thought it was 'the germ of a great
invention,' and advised me to work at it myself. . . . I
added that I felt that I had not the electrical knowledge
necessary to overcome the difficulties. His blunt but
helpful answer was 'Get it.'

285

"I cannot tell you how much these two words have encouraged me. . . . Such an idea as telegraphing vocal sounds would . . . to most minds seem scarcely feasible enough to spend time in working over. I believe . . . that it is feasible, and that I have the clue to the solution of the problem."

If Bell did not have the "clue," when writing to his parents, it was discovered by accident in June 1875. On this eventful day in the history of the telephone, Bell and his assistant, Mr. Watson, were at work trying to send three messages at one time over one wire. Watson was in one room, and Bell in another. Each had three instruments. Each instrument was composed of an electromagnet and a vibrating steel used for an armature.

Bell completed the electric circuit connecting the instruments, and plucked the reed of instrument A. "I asked Watson," said Bell afterwards, "whether his instrument A responded. He said: 'No; the armature of A sticks to the magnet. . . .' I called to him to pluck it loose. It so happened that I had my eyes upon my instrument A, and when he plucked it loose, I saw the armature of my instrument A get into vigorous vibration. I thought that was strange, so I called to Watson, 'Pluck it again.'. . . Well, we did not do anything all that day but pluck reeds. . . . Why did we pluck those reeds all that day? It was proof that the wave-like current produced by the vibration of an armature in front of an electromagnet was powerful enough to produce practical effects. The telephone I had had in mind since the summer of 1874 was really a practical thing. I instantly gave instructions to have the first telephone made."

June was a busy and feverish month for both Watson and Bell. Everything about a membrane electric-speaking telephone had to be learned. Experiments were made to find out whether the best results could be obtained with permanent magnets at each end of the line or with electromagnets. Tests were made with armatures of different thickness and size. Different ways were tried of fastening the armature to a thin piece of skin, which was used for the membrane. The different parts were put together now in this way and now in that way. At least two unsuc- cessful instru- ments were made. Finally the third instrument was ready for trial.

BELL'S CENTENNIAL RECEIVER

The same instrument was used both as a transmitter and as a receiver. That is, one would speak into the instrument and then place his ear to it to hear what was said in reply.

The trial was made in a noisy electrical workshop. Bell was upstairs with one instrument, and Watson was downstairs with another; the two instruments were connected in an electric circuit. Of this trial Bell says: "I spoke, and shouted, and sang into the instrument upstairs. Presently Mr. Watson came upstairs in a state of great excitement. He said: 'I hear your voice; I could almost understand what you said!' I said: 'Try for me.' He tried for me, but I could not hear him. There was no doubt about it, that he could hear something that I said, but I could not very well make out what he said. . . . I could account for the trouble. In the first place, we were in a noisy workshop. My ears, not being accustomed to that noisy workshop, were not so good as his. I was an elocutionist and knew how to throw out my voice; he was a mechanic who did not know. So I could speak better than he could, while he could hear better than I could. I had faith that the instruments were all right, and it turned out that they were. We tried the instruments in a quiet place and they worked all right."

Exhibiting the Telephone

Bell was granted a patent on his telephone on March 6, 1876. He was then twenty-nine years of age, and the

An artist's sketch of Mr. Watson rushing in to Alexander Graham Bell after hearing his voice by telephone in another room.

possessor of what turned out to be the "most valuable single patent ever granted."

Mr. Hubbard, Bell's friend and future father-in-law, had charge of the educational exhibit of the Centennial Exposition, in 1876. He persuaded Bell to exhibit his multiple telegraph and telephone. The telephone transmitter — the part one speaks into — that Bell sent to Philadelphia was made like the transmitter he and Watson had used in their trial of July 1875. But the form had

DOM PEDRO AND THE TELEPHONE

been changed so that one could speak into the tube with greater ease, and could more easily throw the voice directly against the membrane. They had also learned by experience, that one could understand better what was said, if a different instrument was used as a receiver — the part that is held to the ear. So Bell made what came to be known as the iron-box receiver; one of these was also sent to Philadelphia. In the iron-box receiver, instead of employing a thin piece of skin for the membrane, as was done in the transmitter, a thin circular piece of iron was used. With the iron-box receiver, it was easy to hear what was said at some little distance from the instrument.

Bell's telephone instruments were at the Centennial a month, but no one paid much attention to them. Then all of a sudden the telephone became the most talked-of article at the great exhibition. The wonderful change came about in this way.

On Sunday, June 25, the electrical instruments were to be shown to the judges. Dom Pedro, Emperor of Brazil, Sir William Thompson, the greatest electrical scientist at that time in the world, and other famous people were to be there. Mr. Hubbard was anxious that Bell should go to Philadelphia and exhibit his instruments himself, but Bell, because of his school work, refused to go.

"Then Mr. Hubbard took an unfair advantage of me," says Bell. "He appealed to a certain young lady to see what she could do to influence me." (The young lady was none other than Mabel Hubbard, whom Bell married a year later.) "I told her that, of course, I would be glad to go, but that it was impossible; that it was right in the midst of my examinations, and it would not be fair to my pupils. She said, 'Well, won't you come down to the station with me?' 'Yes, I will go down to the station, but you need not try to persuade me, as I cannot go.' So we went down to the station and walked up and down the platform. When the train was going off, and when she saw that I was really not going, she too used an unfair advantage. Who can bear to see a young girl weep? I just jumped on that train. I did not have any baggage or anything else. So, growling like a bear, I went to Philadelphia . . . .

"On Sunday I went out to the exhibition. There were a whole lot of electrical exhibits to be shown . . . and the poor judges were trotted around to see one thing after another until they were fairly ready to drop. I followed the judges around, while they looked at this thing and that thing. They came finally to an exhibit of Elisha Gray, who had a machine for transmitting musical tones like my multiple telegraph. He gave a very interesting talk. It was very interesting to me, because I came next, and he kept on and kept on, until at last, when he got through, the chairman of the judges said they would postpone the further examination of electrical apparatus to another day. That meant that they would never see the telephone. . . . I could only stay that Sunday, and I felt that my whole exhibit was cut out. The judges began to disperse, when suddenly Emperor Dom Pedro saw me, and recognized me as the young man whom he had met in Boston, when he visited the school for the deaf and dumb. He came up to me and said, 'Mr. Bell, how are the deaf-mutes in Boston?' I told him they were very well, and that my exhibit was the next. He said he must go see it, took my arm and walked off with me, and of course the judges followed like a flock of sheep. My exhibit was saved."

The instruments were ready for use. Dom Pedro took a seat at a table on which rested the little iron-box receiver, and was asked to hold his ear near the top of the strange little instrument. Bell sat down in another room and spoke slowly and with great distinctness into the tube of the transmitter. Dom Pedro, of course, did not know what to expect, nor did anyone else in the room, Suddenly the Emperor raised his head and with a look of utter amazement on his face exclaimed, "It talks!" Then came Sir William Thompson, who knew so much about electricity; he listened, and listened, and listened to that little iron disk talk with a human voice. Then with great emphasis said, "It does speak. It is the most wonderful thing I have seen in America. . . . It is the greatest marvel hitherto achieved by the electric telegraph. . . . Before long, friends will whisper their secrets over the electric wire!"

When Sir William Thompson spoke, the world believed.

"I went to bed the night before," said Bell, "an unknown man, and awoke to find myself famous. I owe it to Sir William Thompson, and also to Dom Pedro, and the deaf-mutes of Boston."

Many improvements have been made to the telephone

since the days of Mr. Bell. Various discoveries in the area of electronics and science in recent years have even permitted the use of phones that do not need to be attached to cords or wires. However, the basic principles discovered by Alexander Graham Bell regarding the way sounds travel electronically are still valid today and the importance of Bell's discovery is still universally recognized.

Comprehension Questions

1. In what year was the telephone invented?
2. Where was Alexander Graham Bell born?
3. In what way did Mr. Bell help deaf children?
4. What was the name of Mr. Bell's assistant inventor?
5. Who was Dom Pedro?

A MODERN TELEPHONE

PART IV

Famous Inventors of the Twentieth Century

Chapter 13

Thomas A. Edison

Thomas Alva Edison, nicknamed "The Wizard of Menlo Park," is perhaps the best-known inventor in American history. As a boy, his curiosity and daring led him into unusual adventures, and many interesting stories are told about his boyhood days. These stories often tell about how he pulled a duck off her nest and sat on the eggs himself to see if he could hatch them; how he set fire to a barn, and was publicly whipped for it in the village square; how he tried to read all the books in the public library, and actually read all on a seven-foot shelf; how he set fire, when a newsboy, to a car, and was boxed on the ear by the train conductor, making him deaf for life; how he saved the life of an operator's son, and was taught telegraphy by the operator. All young people should read at least one book on the life of Edison.

OPERATOR TEACHING YOUNG EDISON TELEGRAPHY

During his lifetime, Edison took out about fourteen hundred patents in the United States alone. He did not make all of these inventions himself. He worked like other inventors in his early days, doing all the work himself on whatever he had in hand, but for many years he conducted a great factory in New Jersey, in which hundreds of men were employed, all busy on inventions. Just as other men conduct factories to manufacture, for example, automobiles, Edison conducted his factory to develop inventions. Most of the inventions attributed to him were, therefore, the product of his factory, rather than of himself alone.

The first patent taken out by Edison was in 1869, on a

vote-recording machine. The machine was designed to secure privacy in voting, and to prevent fraud in public elections. The politicians did not want any such machine to come into general use, and the voters were not ready for it, so his first invention proved a flat failure. Edison, however, gained a valuable lesson from this experience. He resolved never to make an invention which was not wanted, and which could not be made a commercial success. From that day on, Edison would not begin a project until after he studied with great care the possible demand for it, the cost of making the invention, and the probable profits from its manufacture and sale. This method of planning work contributed to his commercial success. But no small part of it was due to his industry and to his courage. He worked as hard as any of the men he employed, often toiling for long periods, eighteen out

EDISON'S FAMOUS HORSESHOE PAPER-FILAMENT LAMP, 1870

of the twenty-four hours of the day. Mr. Edison once told a friend that the formula for successful inventing is "one part inspiration and nine parts perspiration." Then, too, it requires courage to invest great sums of money in new and untried things. The fine courage which sustained him during his great career was well illustrated when a great fire destroyed a number of his factory buildings. His answer to the wild flames as they leaped upon and ate up building after building was, "We will begin rebuilding tomorrow."

Of all Edison's inventions, in some ways the most valuable are his electric light, his phonograph, and his moving picture.

When Edison first exhibited his talking machine, in 1877, people hearing it repeat "Mary had a little lamb" thought that it was a greater invention even than the telephone, and crowds filled large halls to hear the wonderful machine. The story went about at the time, that Edison gained the idea of the phonograph from accidentally pricking his finger. This is, of course, not true. The talking machine was the product of careful thought and hard work.

Edison first began to think of reproducing sounds mechanically, from reflecting on the record made on a

Thomas A. Edison

Edison National Historic Site

Thomas Edison in front of his tinfoil phonograph.

disk by a needle attached to a telegraph key. From working with a phonautograph, the instrument used by Bell to record sound waves on a smoked paper, he conceived the idea of recording sounds on tin foil or on a wax disk, and then sending the needle back over the grooves to reproduce the sounds.

AN EARLY MOVING-PICTURE MACHINE

A phonograph is really only a phonautograph developed. The sounds to be reproduced are first recorded in grooves on a wax disk, by means of a phonautograph with a needle attached to the diaphragm. To reproduce the sounds that were recorded, the needle of the phonautograph is sent back over the grooves in the disk, and the sounds produced by the vibrating diaphragm are magnified by a horn-like arrangement. The phonograph is therefore a very simple mechanical invention to reproduce sound. It is, nevertheless, one of the most popular of modern inventions, as it has brought the music of the masters within the reach of the home, at a small cost.

The moving picture, on the other hand, has done in part for the eye what the phonograph has done for the ear. As with some other great inventions, a popular toy was the forerunner of the moving picture. Some twenty years or more before the phonograph was invented, it was possible to buy pictures of boys, in different positions, on a strip of paper stretched over a circular framework. By turning the crank the pictures were whirled around, making the boys appear to be playing leapfrog.

The first real moving pictures were of animals taken in motion. In working with these animal pictures, it was discovered that if they were passed before the eye at the rate of sixteen a second, the eye did not see sixteen pictures of the same animal in different positions, but an animal that appeared to be moving. The moving picture is therefore nothing more than a number of pictures of the same object, animal, or person, in different positions, passed rapidly before the eye. The common rate of taking the pictures and of exhibiting them is sixteen per second. Edison took advantage of this peculiarity of our sight. He perfected the process of taking pictures of objects in motion, discovered the best materials for films, and worked out other practical details essential to good moving pictures. Few towns are now too small to have their movie theater. Probably no invention is more popular, and very few contribute more to the amusement of the public with the possible exception of television.

Electric Lights

At the time when the oil lamp was being improved, a number of scientists were attempting to make a lamp that would be fed by electricity. Thomas A. Edison was one of them. Edison made a glass bulb, put a loop of platinum wire in it, pumped all the air out, and sealed up the tube

Edison invented the electric light in October, 1879

air-tight. Then he ran an electric current through the wire, and it gave a bright, steady light. The trouble with the lamp, however, was that it cost too much, for platinum wire is very valuable. Finally Edison discovered that he could use a fine thread of cotton instead of the wire. As cotton could be obtained at no great cost he was able to make light bulbs very cheaply. In 1882 New York City began using Edison's lights to brighten their streets. In a short time a great industry grew up that required thousands of workers; for cities, towns, and private houses were now lighted with electric lamps.

Edison, however, is to be thought of not only as an inventor, but also as a business man. Around and about his many inventions have grown great business enterprises, of which he was part owner. Thanks to the original business enterprises of Edison, thousands of people are employed by organizations such as record companies, electric power companies, and the movie industry. To have set in motion such gigantic business enterprises, to say nothing of his great contributions to the comfort, pleasure, and amusement of nations, is in itself enough to rank Edison among the most distinguished inventors in American history.

FIRST MOTION PICTURE OF AN OPENING FLOWER

Chapter 14

Orville and Wilbur Wright

People have always had a desire to fly. The first man who tried seriously to learn how to fly was a German named Lilienthal. He built a wing-shaped machine. With this fastened securely under his arms, he would make a running start and glide from the top of high hills or tall buildings. He thus worked for five years, studying how to master air currents and the difficulties of flight, but he never succeeded in floating more than a few minutes at a time. One day, when floating about fifty feet from the ground, his strange machine was caught by a sudden gust of wind, which hurled it to the ground, killing Lilienthal.

Another pioneer of aerial flight was an American, Professor Langley, of the Smithsonian Institution. Although he gave the latter years of his life to the study of this subject, and actually constructed a power-driven machine, he never succeeded in flying more than three-quarters of a mile at any one time.

Professor Langley's experiments, however, attracted much

attention, and French and English scientists with the finest technical training began to work on the problem of aerial navigation. But the first to succeed in flying in a heavier-than-air, power-driven machine were two American young men, with only a high school education, with no scientific training, and with very little money to carry on their work. These two men were Orville and Wilbur Wright.

The Wright brothers were born at Dayton, Ohio. They were always interested in mechanical things, and owned and conducted a successful shop for the repair of bicycles. Their attention was first called to the flying machine by reading, in 1896, of the death of Lilienthal. They began to work on a flying machine as a mere hobby.

They had no money to spend on experiments, nor did they care to risk their lives in trying to fly before they knew how. Accordingly they spent much time in watching birds fly, and in discussing the principles of flight. They read all the books they could find on the subject, and studied all the different flying machines that had been made.

The first flying craft constructed by the Wright brothers — and they always made their own machines — was a glider, which they flew like a kite. It was controlled by levers worked from the ground by ropes. They were thus

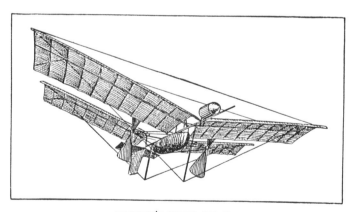

LANGLEY'S STEAM MODEL

able to study the principles of flight, and how to control a flying machine suspended in the air.

Their next machine was a man-carrying glider, which they used, much as Lilienthal had done, to glide in the air from high hills. It was easy enough to glide along on the air, but it was very difficult to balance the glider and to control its course. In order to experiment safely, they went in 1900 to a secluded place in North Carolina, where there were high sand hills that offered good opportunities for gliding, and a soft place on which to land, should they fall. During the next two years, they made about a thousand gliding flights, some of them as far

THE FIRST WRIGHT GLIDER

LILIENTHAL'S WING-SHAPED GLIDER

THE SECOND WRIGHT GLIDER

as six hundred feet.

Their next step was to find a way to propel the glider. During 1903 they were busy on a suitable gasoline motor, but it was not until December that they were ready for their first attempt to fly in a motor-propelled machine. For the trial trip, they went again to the secluded place in North Carolina. The brothers were confident that their machine would fly, but they made no predictions, and had little to say.

"The first flight lasted only twelve seconds, a flight very

modest compared with that of birds, but it was, nevertheless, the first in the history of the world, in which a machine carrying a man had raised itself by its own power into the air in free flight, had sailed forward on a level course without reduction of speed, and had finally landed without being wrecked. The second and third flights (the same day) were a little longer, and the fourth lasted fifty-nine seconds, covering a distance of eight hundred and thirty-five feet over the ground against a twenty-mile per hour wind."

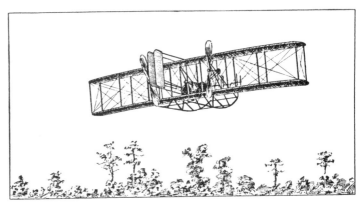

THE WRIGHT AIRSHIP IN FLIGHT

What had started as a hobby soon developed with the Wright brothers into a serious scientific study. By 1905, they had perfected the motor to the point that they were able to make a flight of twenty-four miles, at the rate of thirty-five miles an hour. Up to this time they had worked in comparative quiet, and without being written up in the newspapers and magazines. But their long flights now began to attract the attention of the world.

THE WRIGHT AËROPLANE

In 1908 Wilbur took a machine to France. The French newspapers printed cartoons of him, with a long neck, a beak, and talons for fingers; they also made fun of his shabby-looking machine. Nevertheless, this same Wilbur was not long in breaking the world's record, with a flight of fifty-two miles, being in the air ninety-one minutes. A few days later he won a prize of twenty thousand francs. In addition to this, the French government soon afterwards gave the Wrights an order for thirty machines.

At the very time that Wilbur was breaking world records and winning prizes in France, Orville was making famous flights at Fort Myer, Virginia, flying for more than an hour at a time, and repeatedly ascending with a passenger.

The summer of 1909 witnessed the greatest triumphs in aerial navigation. Bleriot, a Frenchman, crossed the English Channel in his monoplane. Soon afterwards, Zeppelin sailed two hundred and twenty miles in his dirigible balloon, and Orville Wright carried a passenger from Fort Myer to a point in North Carolina. An American airplane, the NC-4, was the first flyer to cross the

NC-4, AMERICAN AIRPLANE, FIRST TO CROSS THE ATLANTIC

ENGLISH DIRIGIBLE R-34, THE FIRST TO CROSS THE ATLANTIC

ocean, in 1919. America's love affair with flight had finally taken off and the world would never be quite as big as it once seemed.

Aircraft are now a regular part of the equipment of all armies, and pilots are able to perform almost unbelievable feats in jet aircraft that fly faster than the speed of sound. The commercial aircraft industry developed during the 1920s and now flies ordinary people to all parts of the world by the thousands each day.

There is something thrilling about riding in an airplane

and making a highway of the air. But the first successful aircraft was perfected, as we have seen, by the Wright Brothers, two unromantic Americans who never allowed themselves to be carried away by their enthusiasm. They never talked about themselves or boasted about what they were going to do. They avoided notoriety and claimed no genius for themselves, yet their quiet and persistent work counted in the end, and they are sure of a place of honor in the history of aerial navigation. The same principles of flight that were discovered by the Wright Brothers, have guided modern aircraft designers and the people who run our nation's space program.

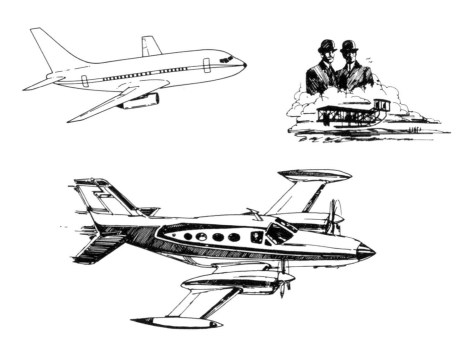

Chapter 15

Guglielmo Marconi

On January 23, 1909, the world suddenly discovered that a wonderful, new, and practical invention had come into use. At daybreak on that day in January the passenger steamer *Republic* collided with the *Florida*, off the coast of Nantucket Island. The *Republic* sent out this message: "We were struck by an unknown boat; engine room filled; passengers all safe; can stay afloat." Instantly the message was caught by the *Baltic*, the *Lorraine*, and by two United States Coast Guard cutters, and all sent their promise to help. The *Baltic* arrived beside the *Republic* first, and saved the lives of sixteen hundred passengers.

But how could a vessel far out in the ocean send a message? By wireless telegraphy, perfected by Guglielmo Marconi. Only eight years before this collision between the *Republic* and the *Florida*, Marconi and an assistant sat at a table in a bare room in the Old Barracks at Signal Hill, Newfoundland. By the side of Marconi hung a telephone receiver connected with a wire, which ran out of the window to a kite, floating four hundred feet overhead. Two thousand miles away, on the coast of Cornwall, England, there sat another man at the foot of a mast two hundred and ten feet high, with a wire hanging down from it connected with an electric battery and a telegraph key.

Marconi cabled to Cornwall that all was ready, then he listened, with the telephone receiver to his ear, for more than a half hour before he heard the first click. There were three of these, meaning "S",

A WIRELESS OPERATOR

the signal he had agreed upon with the man at Cornwall. More signals came, and he listened again and again to make sure. This was the first wireless message over the ocean, and Marconi knew that his invention, upon which he had worked for years, could be made a success.

Marconi was an Italian. He received a splendid scientific training in the schools of Florence and Bologna, and showed an interest in electricity from the time he was twelve years old. One day, when he was about twenty-one, while sending electric waves through the air and

In 1895 Marconi experimented with the first wireless

getting signals a mile away, he accidentally noticed that an instrument on the opposite side of a hill from the sending instrument was affected. The only way this instrument could be affected was by the electric waves passing through the hill. "If electric waves will pass through a hill, they can be made," he said to himself, "to pass long distances over the land and even over the ocean, and it will be possible to telegraph without wires." Thus was born the idea of the wireless telegraph.

Everybody knows that a stone dropped into a pond starts waves in all directions, and although the water only moves up and down, the waves go on and on, until they reach the shore of the pond or have spent their force. In like manner, when a current of electricity is discharged into the air, electric waves go out in all directions and keep on going until their force is spent.

To send a wireless message, an instrument is needed to produce the electric waves, which is called a transmitter; and an instrument to collect these waves, called a receiver.

In the construction of instruments for a wireless telegraph station, the receiver is much harder to make than the transmitter. The most important parts are the coherer, which catches the electric waves, and the decoherer, which makes and breaks the current, producing sounds corresponding to the dots and dashes of the Morse key. The receivers on these early machines were so tuned or harmonized that they received electric waves only from a particular transmitter. In this way, messages were sent as secretly by wireless as by the ordinary telegraph. There are, however, signals which all receivers will catch, like the S O S, used by the wireless to call for help on the high seas.

Several years after Marconi invented the wireless, it was modified and improved in such a way that human speech could be captured and sent out over the air waves to a special receiver. This new feature created a kind of wireless telephone, for people could now receive messages simply by listening to their tiny receiver. This discovery led to the birth of radio.

Even before the sinking of the *Titanic*, most ships were provided with wireless. Since then, all vessels sailing from American ports, and carrying fifty passengers or more, are required by law to be provided with a radio receiver/transmitter. The radio has added greatly to the safety of ocean travellers, and it is extensively used in war and peace.

By 1925 the radio became widely used and respected

around the world. This resulted in a major decline in the use of the older telegraph invented by Mr. Morse. The world could now communicate faster and better, without the use of wires, because of the contributions of Guglielmo Marconi.

Chapter 16

John L. Baird and the Invention of the Television

Not long after Marconi discovered how to send electrical messages without a wire, inventors began to experiment with a system that would send electrical images or pictures through the air.

The invention of the television was, like most inventions, due in large measure to the tireless efforts of several individuals. Briefly, television functions by breaking down images or pictures into millions of tiny dots that can

be translated into electric currents, which then appear on a special screen that can accept the tiny electrical impulses. Few people realize, as they view the images on their television screen, that these images are actually made up of millions of tiny dots that contain various shades of color and brightness. It is the contrast between these different dot formations that provides the viewer with a distinct image on the picture screen.

The first successful television transmission before a public audience was performed by John L. Baird in 1926 as electrically transmitted moving pictures were flashed onto a picture screen. These first public demonstrations encouraged many inventors from Europe and the United States to begin making practical improvements in the quality and function of television transmissions.

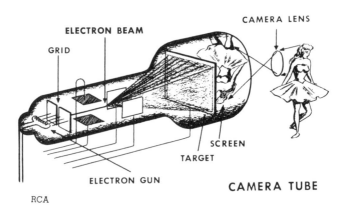

ELECTRON BEAM

GRID

CAMERA LENS

SCREEN

TARGET

ELECTRON GUN

CAMERA TUBE

RCA

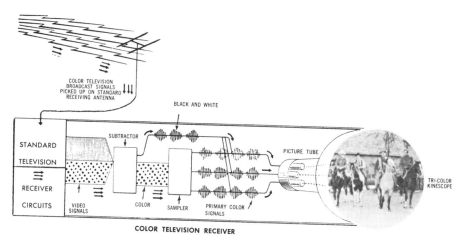

COLOR TELEVISION RECEIVER

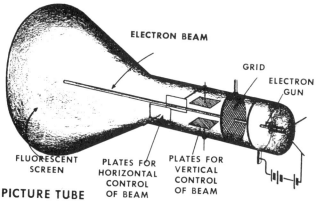

PICTURE TUBE

By the 1950s, the television had improved to the point that millions of sets were being sold each year in the United States and abroad. Today we continue to see improvements in television technology and rarely find a home that does not contain at least one television set. Color television became available to the general public in the 1960s.

It was during the 1970s that the home television set took on new roles with the introduction of various accessories and attachments. Home video cassette recorders and videodisc players freed the viewer from the restrictions of broadcast schedules. Video game attachments provided a new means of entertainment, while home computer systems made the set's screen part of a data-processing system. Home video cameras, used for making tapes to be shown on the set, began to replace conventional film cameras as a means for making home movies.

Needless to say, the invention known as the television has created a communications revolution. The people of the world no longer have to wait days or weeks to receive reports about world or community events. The radio and television now provide people with news and information on almost a constant basis, and people do not need to leave home to get it.

Although the television has demonstrated that it has great potential to increase the knowledge and awareness of people, it has more often been used as a tool of manipulation and social revolution. The tremendous power that television communication has to influence and ultimately change people's world views and moral convictions has been well recognized for many years. Therefore, it is the duty of every citizen to help control the quality of programming that is sent out over the television. In addition, Christian people must carefully choose which programs to view so they do not find themselves falling prey to some of the false and anti-Christ philosophies that occasionally appear on television.

JOHN P. HOLLAND

Chapter 17

John P. Holland and the Submarine

You will remember that Robert Fulton experimented for a long time on a submarine or plunging boat. He believed that his diving boat, the *Nautilus*, with the aid of torpedoes, would make war vessels useless, and so do away with every kind of warfare on the seas. He failed in turn to interest the French, the English, or the United States government in his project, or his boat.

Who first thought of an undersea boat, nobody knows. It certainly was not Fulton, for David Bushnell was floating about New York Bay in the days of the Revolutionary War, in his primitive submarine, the *Turtle*. This boat, so named because it resembled a turtle, floating tail downward and with a conning tower for a head, was literally a one-man boat. It was propelled by two "oars" or "screws" worked from the inside by a crank, and the operator directed its course by means of a rod attached to the rudder, which he held under his arm.

This absurd little submarine, however, came near blowing

up the British frigate *Eagle*, as she lay at anchor with her guns trained on Manhattan Island. On the after deck of the *Turtle* were two hollowed-out pieces of oak filled with gunpowder, arranged to explode, after the operator had bored a hole in the frigate, had deposited his crude torpedoes, and was far enough away to be out of range. But the *Eagle* was copper sheathed, and it was impossible to bore into the hull. Two other attempts were made to blow up British ships with the aid of Bushnell's boat, but both failed. The boat finally came to a sad end, when a sloop carrying her sank, submarine and all. We have David Bushnell to thank, however, for the idea of the conning tower and the propeller, and the actual beginnings of the torpedo.

The War Between the States in America aroused new interest in the submarine. The *Hundley*, operating in Charleston harbor, actually torpedoed and sank the *Housatonic*, but the rush of water from the exploding torpedo sank the *Hundley* with all her crew. So the first victim of the submarine, and the first under sea boat to sink a warship prior to 1914, lay side by side at the bottom of the sea.

The first man to succeed in making a workable and useful submarine was John P. Holland, who was born in Ireland in the year 1842.

John P. Holland

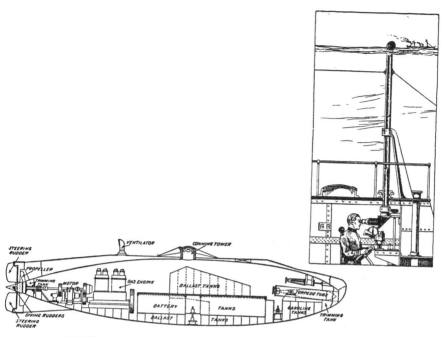

SECTION OF THE HOLLAND SUBMARINE OF 1901

Holland was busy on an under sea boat in 1862. On coming to Paterson, New Jersey, in 1873, where he became a teacher, he continued to work away at his plan after school hours. He built altogether seven submarines, none of which amounted to much. Finally, in 1898, he launched the *Holland No. 8*. This was a porpoise-like craft, fifty-three feet long and ten feet wide, with a single torpedo tube. It plunged head on, like a duck, when water was let into specially arranged compartments, and it rose to the surface when the water was driven out by compressed air — all in five seconds. It could be held at any desired depth under water, where it moved about like a fish. When afloat it had a speed of eight miles an hour, and a cruising radius of 1500 miles. After seeing the *Holland,* Admiral Dewey said, "If they (the Spaniards) had two of these things at Manila, I could not have held it."

Within the next few years, Holland sold plans for submarines to the United States, England, Japan, and Germany.

The nuclear-powdered submarines in use at present are often over 300 feet long, with crews of from one to two hundred men. They cross and re-cross the oceans of the world with ease and are not required to surface. Modern submarines are much different from the primitive versions that came out in the early 1900s.

These early submarines rode on the surface of the water with their heavy oil-burning engines at a rate of twenty to thirty miles an hour. When submerged, electricity was used, because it made less heat and threw off fewer odors to pollute the air, which had to be safeguarded, lest the crew suffocate. These submarines could only remain under water twenty-four hours at a time, but to be comfortable for the crew, they needed to come to the surface five or six times a day, to pump in a supply of fresh air.

Submarines no longer dive straight down. After everything is shut tight to keep out the water, the bow of the submarine is tipped slightly, and the boat glides gently down to the desired depth. Fifty feet is the ordinary depth, but they can dive to a depth of several hundred feet. Submerging is more or less dangerous, however, and frightful accidents have occurred. Something may go wrong with the machinery. Or if they dive too deep the great pressure of the sea may crush the hull. Or, as happened with the American F-4, when the entire crew was lost, acids from the electric batteries may eat away the rivets so that the hull may cave in.

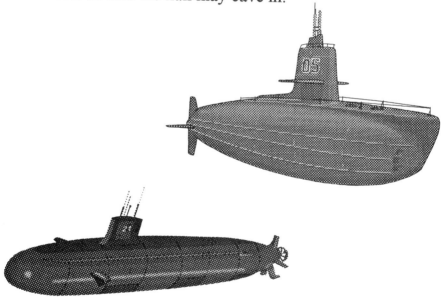

The latest submarines have both eyes and ears. The eye is the periscope, so necessary to submergence. The periscope consists of a system of mirrors inside a tube, which is extended, when the boat is submerged, to a distance of fifteen to twenty feet above the surface of the water. By looking into the mirror at the bottom of the periscope, the captain sees everything that happens above. The periscope thus enables the submarine to locate ships, and to aim its deadly torpedoes without unnecessary exposure. Modern submarines often have the ability to fire nuclear missiles at enemy targets without having to come to the surface at all.

When afloat, a radio outfit serves for ears. But submarines can also hear when under water. A steel disk is attached to the hull, and this disk, by means of an electric current, acts as an under-sea wireless. The steel ear has still another use. The engines of vessels in motion make considerable noise. This is carried through the water and vibrates the submarine's ear. After a little practice it is easy for the listener to tell the direction from which the noise comes, and the locality of the ship. The device is known as sonar.

The submarine is thus a monster that dives, and floats, and moves with animal-like quickness; that sees, and hears, and has mile-long arms of more than giant strength.

John P. Holland

Comprehension Questions

1. What type of invention did Mr. Edison take out his first patent for?
2. What invention repeated the words "Mary had a little lamb?"
3. Who invented the electric light?
4. How did the Wright brothers make a living while they worked on the airplane?
5. What invention was Guglielmo Marconi responsible for developing?

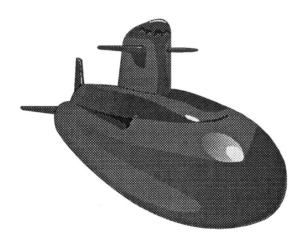

The Story of Inventions

A PICTURE-MAP OF THE MOON: A DEAD WORLD LIT UP BY THE SUN

This is a picture-map of the moon, which is really a dead world, as the earth would be if there were not one living thing upon it. The moon travels round the earth as the earth travels round the sun. It is not light in itself; what we see is the light of the sun upon it, like the light of a candle thrown upon a wall. We see really one half of an enormous globe, like a small earth, lit up in the sunshine, spinning in space like a fireball, yet weighing millions of tons. The little map shows how much bigger than Great Britain the moon is.

334

Chapter 18

Wernher Von Braun and Rockets to the Moon

One of the most exciting developments in the twentieth century was the dawn of the space age. For centuries man had dreamed of inventing a spacecraft that could take him into outer space. However, during the 1960s the dream of space exploration became a reality.

Rockets operate in direct accordance with the *Third Law of Motion*. The *Third Law of Motion* states simply that every action is accompanied by an equal but opposite reaction. It is the *Third Law of Motion* that gives a rifle its kick when the trigger is pulled. The action of the bullet, moving forward, causes the gun to move backward with equal force.

Because rockets work so directly in accordance with the *Third Law*, they can operate even better in space than in the atmosphere. The rocket needs no air to push against. The impulse that drives it forward comes from within itself. An airplane, which needs air to support its wings, to spin its propeller, and to pass through its jets, would be helpless without the atmosphere.

First Rocket Ships

During the 19th century, rocket theories were far-fetched and fantastic. Some of the designs inventors drew then looked more like paper darts than actual rocket ships. Outside of war rockets, no real progress was made. And war rockets were found to be no match for quick firing artillery.

It was not until 1920 that real rocket-ships began to make progress. In that year, an American, Dr. Robert H. Goddard, a professor at Clark College in Worcester, Massachusetts, published a long article. This article told of the possibility of using rockets to explore the upper atmosphere, which balloons could not reach.

At the end of his article, Dr. Goddard suggested that it might be possible to build a space-rocket. He proposed to send his space-rocket, packed with magnesium, to the Moon. When it struck the Moon, the rocket would make such a big explosion that astronomers on Earth would be able to see and record the flash.

The Goddard article excited much interest, especially in Germany. Having lost World War I, the Germans were forbidden by treaty to build airplanes of any kind. Naturally, a large number of German scientists turned to the idea of building rockets large enough to carry passengers. Such rockets could be developed by Germany without violating any treaty restrictions.

This movement was given impetus by a book published in 1923, written by a Transylvanian schoolteacher named Oberth. Oberth's book was the first to suggest that human space-flight in rockets might be practical. Quickly, a

German rocket society was founded. Its members not only wrote books about space-ships, but built models and tested them.

Goddard Goes Ahead

In the meantime, Dr. Goddard was going ahead with his own rocket experiments. A private foundation gave him a hundred thousand dollars to continue his work. He moved to New Mexico, not far from the U.S. Government White Sands Rocket Proving Ground. There he tested rocket fuels and found liquid fuels to be far more practical than solid fuels.

Dr. Goddard continued to build bigger and bigger models of space-ships until after Pearl Harbor. Then he went to work for the Navy. He built rocket-boats to back troop landings in the Pacific. Dr. Goddard was still working for the Navy when he died of a throat ailment in 1945. He is known the world over as the father of modern rocketry.

During World War II, a skilled team of German scientists and inventors led by Wernher Von Braun, developed a series of rockets that were primarily utilized for military purposes. These rockets were known as the V-1 and V-2 rockets. It was during the testing and perfecting of these rockets that Von Braun and his staff learned a great deal about flying rockets into space.

At the close of World War II, the defeated German scientists and technicians surrendered to the American army. Most of their V-2 rockets and equipment were moved to America. A short time later, Von Braun was placed in charge of the development of a space/missile program for the United States government.

Some of the problems that this team of scientists had to overcome included how to accurately guide a rocket into space, how to formulate the correct fuel and engine power to lift a heavy rocket into space, and how to communicate with men who are flying in outer space.

Hundreds of experimental rockets were sent into space from 1946 to 1961. Many of these test flights helped to provide scientists with the information needed to overcome the remaining obstacles to sending up a man into outer space.

Finally in 1961, the first American to travel into outer

space and orbit around the earth, Lt. Col. John Glenn, successfully completed his mission. Communication with this manned spacecraft was made possible by two great inventions of the 1940s — the electronic computer and the transistor. The invention of the transistor in 1948 made it possible to reduce the size of electronic units.

The computer helped to track the path of the space craft and the transistors (which have replaced the old-fashioned vacuum tubes) greatly improved radio communications from space because they provided a stronger, smaller and more reliable electrical system for communication

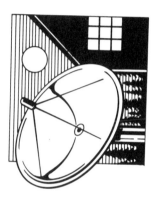

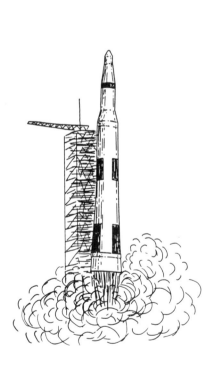

devices. Numerous improvements have been made to both computers and transistors since the 1950s. Modern computers can store and compute a wealth of man-made knowledge. Printed electrical circuits that do not require wires and "chips" that combine several electrical components further revolutionized the field of electronics during the 1960s.

America's space program, guided by Wernher Von Braun, continued to make progress, and in 1963 President John F. Kennedy announced that the United States would try to send a man to the moon before 1970. The Apollo spacecraft with its Saturn V rockets was developed and perfected by Von Braun's team during the 1960s and was specifically designed to carry astronauts to the moon and back.

On July 21, 1969, astronauts Neil Armstrong and Edward Aldrin landed and walked on the moon. A gigantic Saturn V rocket, capable of flying at over 25,000 miles per hour, carried these Americans safely to the moon and back home to earth. In thirteen short years, Wernher Von Braun and his skilled team of workers invented numerous rockets and spacecraft. Thanks to their efforts, and the work of other designers and inventors like Dr. Goddard, the United States was able to realize its dream of space exploration and a moon landing.

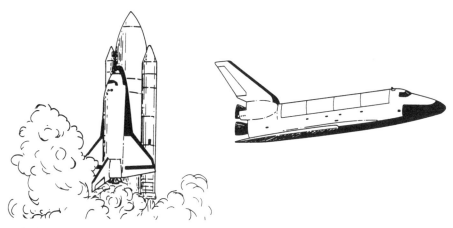

No other nation has ever been able to send men to the moon and return them safely to earth. America's space program has continued to grow over the years. In 1981, the United States developed a special reusable spacecraft known as a space shuttle. This craft can carry several astronauts into outer space and return to earth in the same manner as a regular airplane. Therefore, the space shuttle can be used over and over again.

During the later part of his career, Dr. Wehrner Von Braun took the time to express his personal belief in God and eternal life. His statements help to remind us that many of the great inventors and scientists of days gone by were also men and women of faith. Von Braun stated,

> "I believe there are God-ordained principles which move us. One is a belief in a final judgment when every one of us has to

account for what we did with God's great gift of life on earth. In our modern world, people seem to feel that science has somehow made such 'religious ideas' seem old-fashioned. Nevertheless, I think science has a real surprise for the skeptics. Science, for instance, tells us that nothing in nature, not even the tiniest particle, can disappear without a trace. Think about that for a moment. Nature does not know extinction, only change. Now if God applies this fundamental principle to the most tiny and humble parts of the universe, doesn't it make sense to assume that He also applies it to the masterpiece of His creation — the human soul? I think it does.

Everything science has taught me, and continues to teach me, strengthens my belief in the continuity of our existence after death."

Comprehension Questions

1. What were the names given to the first rockets developed by Wernher Von Braun?
2. Who was the first astronaut to orbit the earth in a spacecraft?
3. How did the computer and the transistor help to promote space travel?
4. What man was put in charge of America's space program from 1946-1970?
5. How has the invention of the space shuttle helped make space travel more practical?

Chapter 19

The Invention of the Computer

During the 1950's a revolution was beginning in America. This revolution had its beginnings many years earlier and will impact the entire world for many years to come. The revolution that we will be looking at started with the invention of the first electronic computer.

The computer had its beginnings in the 1600s. A French mathematician named Blaise Pascal invented a

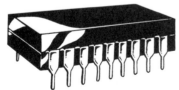

mechanical calculating machine in 1642. It used gears, wheels, and cylinders to add and subtract numbers. As he could not get the fine machined parts he needed, his machine did not work properly. Similar manual computers were also invented during this era, but they were all rather clumsy and useless. It was not until the twentieth century, with advancements in the use of electricity, that a practical computer could be developed.

In 1940, Dr. Howard Aiken and International Business Machines developed the first calculator that used electricity to operate. It relied on the mechanical action of relays to perform computations, and as a result it was very slow.

Prior to 1940, a computer was a person who did computations for a living. Computers were employed by the military to calculate firing tables so that our troops fighting in Europe during World War II would know how to best aim their big guns for different conditions and distances.

These calculations by human computers took a lot of time. Too much time for modern fast-paced warfare. The United States Army set out to find a way to calculate faster. They turned to the University of Pennsylvania for help. Professor John Mauchly and one of his students, J. Presper Eckert, invented their first computer, named ENIAC (Electronic Numeric Integrator and Calculator) to calculate firing tables. This computer was completed too late to shorten the war, but it did start the computer revolution.

This computer used a new technology, the vacuum tube. The vacuum tube was used in place of the relays of earlier calculating machines. A relay computer could perform about 10 additions per second, but an early vacuum tube computer could perform about 5000 additions per second. This increased speed came at a price: Increased heat, and decreased reliability as vacuum tubes burned out rapidly.

The First Commercial Computer

After World War II, Mauchly and Eckert started the first commercial computer company, with its first contract to supply a computer to the United States Census Bureau to aid with the census. This was the first computer used for business applications. It was called UNIVAC.

The Invention of the Computer

Several commercial computer companies were started during the 1950s. They designed several improvements and developed new computer models. These computers were room-sized machines and needed a small army of people to operate and repair them.

In 1947, Bell laboratories invented the solution to the problems of heat and poor reliability with the invention of the transistor. A transistor performs the same function as a vacuum tube, but it uses less heat, takes up less space, and is highly reliable. As the transistor was used more and more, both the cost and the size of computers decreased.

In 1959, Texas Instruments invented a method which further decreased the size of computers. They discovered how to "grow" transistors onto small pieces of silicon. These pieces are called a "chip." Using this technology, scientists are able to make computers so small that they can fit into a briefcase, and have more power than a computer that would have filled an entire room 30 years ago.

God has given us computers to provide many good things for our society. Unfortunately, ungodly men have been using the computer for evil purposes. Grocery stores, for instance, are now encouraging customers to pay by charge card or to use a "check card". This is used, along with the Universal Product Code on each item, to track what each customer buys and how often. Computers are now used regularly to invade our privacy and to gather information about us without our permission. It is up to us to make sure that we use this technology in a godly manner.

Computers received their name from the human computers they first replaced. Today, they do much more than compute. There are computers controlling cars, airplanes, street lights, power plants, military machines, and much more. In fact, this book was typeset on a computer.

Computers have changed our everyday lives to the extent that our society does not function very well when they do not work properly. Signal lights cease to function, cars do not work correctly, and airplanes cannot fly safely without the aid of computers.

Conclusion

It has often been said that "necessity is the mother of invention." In other words, when mankind seeks to stretch its dreams and goals to the limit, it very often motivates creative people to invent the machines that are capable of fulfilling the need at hand. Perhaps this is why most people greatly admire the noble spirit of inventors, people who can see a need of mankind, and are willing to sacrifice themselves in the pursuit of a solution to man's problems. May God always bless the earth with people who are willing to sacrifice themselves in the pursuit of excellence, for the benefit of mankind.

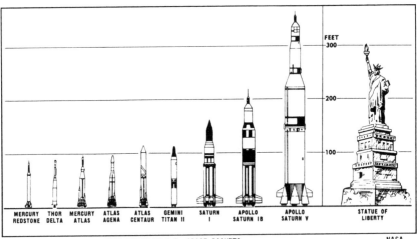

									FEET
MERCURY REDSTONE	THOR DELTA	MERCURY ATLAS	ATLAS AGENA	ATLAS CENTAUR	GEMINI TITAN II	SATURN I	APOLLO SATURN IB	APOLLO SATURN V	STATUE OF LIBERTY

DEVELOPMENT OF U.S. SPACE ROCKETS   NASA